RABINDRANATH TAGORE
DIVERSE DIMENSIONS

MOHIT CHAKRABARTI

ATLANTIC PUBLISHERS & DISTRIBUTORS
4215/1, Ansari Road, Darya Ganj
New Delhi-110002

Published by :

Atlantic Publishers & Distributors
4215/1, Ansari Road, Darya Ganj,
New Delhi-110002

Head Office :

B-2, Vishal Enclave, Najafgarh Road,
New Delhi-110027
Phone : 5413460

Printed at : Print India through Chawla Composers,
Hari Nagar, New Delhi

DEDICATED TO

Swami Lokeswarananda,
Secretary,
The Ramakrishna Mission
Institute of Culture,
CALCUTTA,
to whom I endlessly owe.

PREFACE

The world of Rabindranath Tagore is a world of our very own. The web of eternal curious attitude in man—his inner world and the outer one—is woven in a fine thread of consciousness for which Tagore eternally comes closest to man anywhere and everywhere. *Rabindranath Tagore* : *Diverse Dimensions* is a study of a multi-dimensional personality in quest of the excellence of man.

Education is never given so much importance as it is today. But it has perhaps been completely confused because it is continually losing cordial relationship with having, loving and being. A revaluation of Tagore's educational thoughts and experiments made in the first treatise might show newer avenues.

For a true beyonding of consciousness and partnership with Beauty, man alone can claim excellence. To be conscious of this quest for beyonding and beauty is to nursle the soul of humanity in poignance of perfection. The perfume of these two mystico-aesthetic flowers of excellence may be inhaled in "The Mystic Muse in *Song Offerings*" and "Rabindranath's Quest for Beauty".

The waning years of Tagore are marvels of poetic vision. Pregnant expressions, powerful imageries, poised symbolism, mystic experiences—all these are spread like sparkling pearls in the Poet's immortal creation *Convalescence* (*Arogya*). "Tagore's poetic vision in *Convalescence* (*Arogya*)" is a modest endeavour to explore and appreciate this poetic excellence.

"The World of Tagore's Folk Songs" is a study of Tagore's rediscovery of *maner manush*—the Man of the heart—who sings with an *ektara* in every heart.

How can social change be brought about ? What is the role of education ? What are the avenues for better fusion between education and society ? "Fulness in Education and Social Change : Tagorean Viewpoints" might be an appropriate pointer.

Man today stands at the cross-roads of excellence and extinction. The concept of man blurred, blinded and booed in manifold massacres of modernity, is reassessed in "Tagore's Concept of Man".

"Rabindranath Tagore and Sri Aurobindo : A Quest for Mystic Identities" is a comparative study of the mystic visions of Tagore and Aurobindo, which might invite special interest and attention of esteemed readers in an unusually—and, of course, undesirably—neglected area of critical appreciation.

I would like to express my profound gratitude to Dr. K.R. Gupta of Atlantic Publishers & Distributors for publication of this book.

I am unendingly indebted to Swami Lokeswarananda of the Ramakrishna Mission Institute of Culture, Gol Park, Calcutta, to whom this book is dedicated.

If the book appeals to revered readers and widens Tagoreana towards diverse dimensions, I shall feel myself profusely rewarded.

Seemantika
VISVA-BHARATI UNIVERSITY
SANTINIKETAN-731235

MOHIT CHAKRABARTI

CONTENTS

RELEVANCE OF RABINDRANATH TAGORE'S EDUCATIONAL THOUGHTS AND EXPERIMENTS

Rabindranath rethought is humanity revitalized. The conscience of the modern man is bewildered in blurred visions of humanity. Today no man—let us frankly admit—passes a single moment of serene blessedness. None enjoys a happy, peaceful night to be reawakened with the renewed vigour and pulsating moments of tomorrow. Is today buried in the ruins of tomorrow ? The human conscience awaits a definite answer. And Tagore shows the avenue of excellence.

The wails of humanity are, indeed, the eternal quest of mankind for emergence of good sense and sensibilities. For Rabindranath and for ourselves and for humanity at large, emancipation of conscience from the perils of so called modernity leaves no alternative. Megamachines must make room for the fruits of conscience. Hi-tech phobia must harbour the essence of all-embracing goodness and simplicity in the heartland of mankind. For Tagore, everyone has the immense possibility to be re-enkindled with the conflagration of conscience to contribute as best as possible to the advancement of human civilization.

Admittedly, the lost soul of humanity awaits a worthy revival, a great come back. How can mankind make that mesmeric event possible ? A peerless pointer to the marvels of humanity, Rabindranath redirects mankind to the inner world of conscience. The crisis of civilization as he poignantly feels, is the crisis of conscience. Let all good sense of humanity be directed to eliminate the ills and evils of humanity. Let the arrows of avarice and aggression be burned into blessings of mankind in the form of all round endeavour.

Unendingly optimistic as he was, Tagore always believes in the eternal possibilities of human resources. An individual must remain an individual, and, by remaining as such, must explore and expand his priceless individuality for the goodness of one and all. All his glory and honour is burned into an excellence for the onward march of humanity.

The search for excellence is creative, cautious, critical, continual.

Charaiveti—the search is on.

The birth of man is, as Tagore characteristically thinks, one of individuality. *c'est moi*. Here I am. The 'I' within is the 'I' without, the 'I' that makes a natural encounter with all creatures and all things the good God has magnificently created. As the Poet himself poignantly appeals :

> *More nam ei vale khyata hok*
> *Ami tomaderi lok*
> [Let my name be glorified in the sense that I am your very own.]

(Translated by me)

What a birth ! But, then, the birth necessitates an ardent and thrilling journey—the joyous adventure as anyone might call it—whipping off the riff-raffs of life and shaking hands with whatever is true, good and beautiful. It might, of course, appear that the journey is veering towards a passionate beckoning of romanticism, the land of the most pulsating feeling of contentment, but, even then, all reasonings and shrewd observations that are married to down-to-earth realities of life cannot but heave a sigh of relief through the consciousness of oneself being not shrouded in the mystery of stagnation.

Admittedly, with all moral, social, political, economic and intellectual awakenings along with increasing sense of hopelessness and desolation, the individual is guillotined in the protest-proof arena of silence everywhere. Civilization, as Tagore foresees, is booed in abject mockeries of life. An impenetrable blockade of miseducation reigns almost supreme. Institutions for advancement of learning dole out happy degrees, diplomas and certificates that prove worthless nonsense in moulding an individual to be true and responsible to his 'I'—the greater 'I'. Macabred or massacred is no longer in the waiting list of attributes for a meticulously modernized world where an individual is even now turned into 47A or 69E as Rabindranath so characteristically describes in his play *Red Oleanders*. Whither education and, for that end in view, emancipation of individuality ?

Apart from the fact that an individual cannot but embrace the society to which he belongs, it is equally true that he cannot help doing justice to himself bearing in mind the fact that the life of an individual permeates the process of discovering himself anew to enter deeply into himself until and unless he is enlightened with the true meaning of his very existence, the meaning of life. Essentially, this discards the mere intuition—the so-called abused knowledge often tentamount to the enrichment of individuality in vain—that does not make a desirable go for the higher stratas of education *viz.*, innovation, critical thinking and creativity. The great tragedy of education everywhere is that it caters to the learner only from the point of view of utilitarian ukase and not to the essence of individuality so badly needed for an enlightened society.

With all education centred in and controlled within a limited atmosphere of a mechanical panorama of life, the unmodernly modern man is the ironical product of a reincarnated robot. When finer feelings and softer emotions of life are weighed in the balance of slovenliness and hooliganism in the name of modernity and the distress of being alone is merged in the raging din and bustle of agonies and ecstasies, one might look askance at oneself and ponder over the immense possibilities of mankind being helplessly lost in futility. A shamelessly hollow world with flambuoyant spirit of arms and ammunitions cannot serve as an antidote to the hungry hearts of creative potentialities continually and shabbily ignored in inglorious modernity. The individual, with all avenues open to him, fails to open himself out 'to see', as Wordsworth introspects, 'into the life of things'. The training or education of an individual is nothing but this unfolding of the inner man with this inner vision that substantially contributes to the planning and excellence of life. This is not at all an alien affair in the history of education in India. Evidently, whatever education was imparted in ancient India in the *Tapovan* system of education points to the fact that the unique individuality of a learner must, at any cost, be maintained and must be given ample opportunities to march forward with the untiring spirit of discovery : 'to strive, to seek, to find, and not to yield'. The onward march for self-discovery through education is silenced when an individual's freedom of thought and expression, critical and creative manifestation and the role of his ever-inquisitive spirit of knowing beyond what is known and seeing beyond what is seen and feeling beyond what is felt is dogged in drudgeries and abstractions of life.

Civilization thus pawned in abstractions and passivities awaits a change. Education welcomes this change through the individual excellence of mankind leading to all-round excellence. A true, forceful and dignified individual is one blessed with this excellence.

Unlike any other educational thinker, Rabindranath cares more for poignance and excellence of individuality in education than for anything else. The crisis of civilization is, indeed, the crisis of poignance and excellence of individuality. It is the crisis that calls for revaluation of values and revival of prized individuality. In his essay entitled "Sikshar Herpher" ("Topsy-turvy Education") published in "The Visva-Bharati Quarterly," November 1946—January 1947, Tagore refers to the agonies of doing away with this belief in the infinite spirit of individuality in case of education and appeals fervently for a worthy re-union of education and life :

> We have also the same prayer. If the differences are eliminated, we are contented. We have this appalling poverty because we are failing to make conformity between winter and garments for the winter, summer and garments for the summer. Otherwise everything we have. Now we pray for this boon to the Almighty : synchronize our appetite with food, clothes with seasons, ideas with language and education with life. Our position is like :

Fish athirsty in water
Arousing Volleys of laughter.

seeing that we have both water and thirst, the people of the world are laughing and tears are rolling down from our eyes. Only we are failing to drink.

[Translated by me]

—Rabindranath Tagore : "Sikshar Herpher", *Siksha*, Visva-Bharati 1973, pp. 18-19.

The birth of an individual enriched and purified in the fire of education is one of his potentiality so unique and so eternal that an appeal to all the different sensibilities in him in the right direction would undoubtedly lead him to understand and evaluate the inner truth of individuality. Pawned to apparent priorities and necessities of life, the march is often deterred and camouflaged—a contrived stage of human drama, so to say—but, above all, even the journey alone to foster the spirit of oneness in individuality—a rare and cautiously avoided avenue of marching ahead—is the only desirable spirit to challenge and defer the imminent horror-stricken doom of humanity. Are we attuned to this journey in right earnest ?

THE SEARCH WITHIN

Posed with innumerable encumbrances of the ukase of modernity, the individual faces a challenge—a challenge of an unending search within to find the avenue onward and backward to visualize his own incomparable *cidakas*, the sky of the heart. This visualization not only indicates the fruit of education so effectively nourished and nurtured through maintenance of the true spirit of individuality but it encompasses a cosmic dome of universalized education for oneness, alas, lost in the oblivion of ambiguities of intensive intellectual cold wars. Lost, therefore, is our home for uninterrupted spirit of creating a world of our very own—a world that primarily cares for evolving newer dimensions of individual as well as all-round development of pioneering personality. The man here merges in *men* and *vice versa*, but, then, in each case, the possible avenues are not encountered in a mess of encroachments leading to absence of disinherited spirit of imbalance and incoherence.

Basically a humanist, Tagore breaks new grounds with the signal thought that all practices and experimentations in connexion with education must emphasize the fact that the language of intellect which is often erroneously interpreted in terms of the language of words, words and words alone is primarily learning the language of a multidimensional personality. The man at the back of education often outclassed in social misgivings and political pandemonia is one to be de-educated : perhaps or certainly as it is so throttled in the West as well as in the East, too, to a great extent that many educationists gravely feel the need for de-schooling—a fact not altogether alien in case of Tagorean experiments in education. Torn between the national awakening of education on the one hand and the clerk-oriented education bred in virgin but very vulnerable soil in the yoked India on the other, Rabindranath painfully experienced the sad lot of education directly or indirectly in schools, colleges and universities where advancement of learning is equivalent to the scoring of marks and marks through the parrot's training in rot memorization. Hence, the crisis of character and humanity, the greatest crisis of the crises of civilization. When education becomes an easy prey to commercialization not, of course, an uncommon scene in our country as well as elsewhere, even after an elapse of over four decades of national independence and it can be easily bought by means of aggravated affluence, tension runs riot and delicately creeps in even in the midst of violent protests at almost all centres of learning. What a wailing of uncontrolled controversies and sentimental incompetencies writ large in, for example, failures encompassing universalization of primary education, leaving aside tall talks, high-sounding theories, experimentations and practices in population education, education of the disabled and, last but not the latest nor even the least, environmental education ! Amidst this backdrop of all pervading decadence, the individual is at the cross-roads of looking within and looking for an avenue of enrichment and re-awakening of the spirit of self-learning and self-development. Would one remain deaf to the call and disinterested in the search within ?

The Essence of Rabindranath Tagore's Educational Innovations

A re-thinking of Rabindranath Tagore's educational innovations highlights the following fundamental educational thoughts and experiments that have contributed abundantly to the promotion of education for a changing world :

I. *Education of the whole man*

According to Tagore, the education that is primarily necessary for fulness is education of the whole man. This type of education teaches every learner to conquer his own little self and herald his higher self—the self that by no means betrays his development of personality, considering the fact that self-reliance and self-understanding act as the most precious qualities of personality. The type of education that emboldens one's spirit also teaches one how to ride above petty selfishness, how to be liberal but not unusually and unduly uncompromising to every affair of life and experience and how to feel the pulse of oneness of humanity. It also allows one to be imbued with the spirit of truth that sustains and glorifies the human mind. The education that widens one's outlook and broadens the spirit of unstinted devotion to service to humanity and patriotism fires one with the untiring zeal for tearing off the shackles of all temptations and giving all ears to the call of the indomitable, the endless and the most thrilling adventure of life. Indeed, true education always stands for advancement of erudition of the whole man and progress of world civilization. And all true education is the education of austerity ably nursed, caressed and guided by the strict observance of self-enrichment through self-discipline. In his address to the students delivered on the occasion of the annual convocation ceremony of the university of Calcutta in February 1937 and afterwards published by Visva-Bharati in the form of a booklet, Rabindranath advises them poignantly :

> Leave off the aroma of all temptations. Nurture, like a courageous man, the bright intellect with which you kick off all ugliness as an outcome of irrelevance and accept the responsibities of your country with earnest resolution.
> —Rabindranath Tagore : "Chatrasambhasan", *Siksha*, Visva-Bharati 1973, p. 259.
>
> [Translated by me]

Education of the whole man thus incorporates the idea of universalism whereby the whole world is transformed into a world of true humanity and each country tries to reach the highest point of excellence in every affair of life. Education there allows one to inculcate the spirit of excellence of oneself in homogeneity even under the duress of a heterogeneous atmosphere of life. The sooner one succeeds as a learner in utilizing one's own power of excellence to the cause of any other individual or to the country and the world at large, the better is the possibility of coming out of the wolf of typical human aggressions tearing off the entraits of the spirit of unified sense of oneness.

II. *Education for Individuality*

That true education aims at the emancipation of true individuality is the epitome of Tagore's educational thoughts and experiments. Essentially a romantic, he highlights the spirit of individuality in moulding the overall development of personality. In his letter to Nalin C. Ganguly, later on published in the reputed Bengali monthly, *Pravasi*, Jaistha 1338 B.C. under the caption "Sikshār Sārkathā" ("the Essentials of Education"), he criticises the traditional process of education where the development of one's individuality is sandwitched in the commercial approach to impart education with a view to earning one's bread and never to have an access to the wide world of exercise of individual intellectual excellences.

Again, in his essay titled "Siksha-Samskar" ("Educational Reconstruction") read out by Tagore himself at a meeting convened in the Overtoon Hall, Calcutta on 23 *Jaistha* 1313 B.C. and later on published in the then Bengali journal *Bhandar* in *Asadh* 1313, Rabindranath adroitly sums up the sordid state of affairs of a pupil whose individuality never finds an outlet to be enkindled with erudition and blessed with enjoyment while he is at the threshold of a new domain of learning :

> Our ideas are strengthened when they have been allowed unhindered avenues for manifestation. * * * Knowledge and ideas accepted with one's own intrinsic evaluational

approach that incorporates comparison, contrast and assimilation as tools invite an individual to be more living and more courageous to voice forth one's unique way of thinking than merely accepting thoughts without having any reaction whatsoever. Knowledge judged from the latter kills time and energy and the individual's rich soil of expression remains intellectually virgin, fruitless and drab. Who cares for the peril of intellect and individuality ?

—Rabindranath Tagore : "Siksha-Samskar", *Siksha*, Visva-Bharati, 1973, pp. 34-35.

[Translated by me]

While society aggravates the process of commonalty where mechanized education mars the role of the individual, education cannot but pay a heavy price for all-pervading abstractions. A routine oriented process of education right from the early stage of learning with no room for freedom of expression, allowance of minimum time to encounter the insatiable spirit of originality, promotion of class-consciousness even in learning matters, gagging individual opinions and criticisms, marauding the desirable traits of personality to be involved through reactions, and engulfing the whole arena of the curriculum with short notes, made easies, suggestions, one-night-preparation schedules, last minute exam pull-outs, point-wise blow-ups—well, what more for education-pollution and massacre of individual potentialities ? As a sharp reaction to all these and many other cancerous ills of education, Rabindranath highlights the spirit of individuality and gives top-most priority to growth and development of an individual learner through uninterrupted pursuit of learning. In his own Visva-Bharati what he continually strived for was an uninterrupted and natural atmosphere of exercise of one's individuality in the pursuit of erudition under diverse experiences arrived at through exchange of scholarship and marriage of minds. He also reiterated the fact that in the process of development of individuality, a balance between within and without, between the artificial, narrow, drab and mechanized elements of worldly affairs and the real, wide, wonderful and unique world of one's own in order to find the true meaning of life by means of untiring endeavour must be the objective of education.

III. *Education for Freedom*

With a view to ensuring the individual learner to find out the best in himself, to exercise his own individual potentialities under favourable atmosphere and to be critical and creative from every aspect of erudition, education must, as Rabindranath emphasizes, make room for wider avenues of freedom. Unfortunately this concept of freedom is very often belittled as it is often unjustifiably apprehended that it might contribute to individual eccentricity leading to bewildering and stratified aims of education. Morever, with no common role to stand and voice forth in unity where the interest of all rather than a single learner is involved, education turns into nothingness as it invites multifarious artificial processes of learning with no discipline inherent in them. But, then, the fruits of the individual learner's freedom of thought and expression in course of education vitalizing the development of personality so poorly pawned to generalized streamlined process of education that ends in strengthening the number of millions of frustrated jobless millions can no longer be ignored.

Rabindranath deeply feels that in education this freedom of an individual is the first criterion of creation of consciousness—the consciousness of what one is and that one should be. While as an exponent of advancement of learning through the mother-tongue he holds high the esteemed position of pursuit of learning through one's own language so that the learner might not encounter unusual impediments in the infinite domain of learning and experience, he also states the importance of knowing, receiving, and utilizing the best thoughts, best ideas, best expressions of the alien world by moulding in one's own fashion and enriching with critical and creative contributions. Education is thus raised to the position of identifying, analysing and incorporating freedom right from an individual up to a society. In his essay "Sikshar Swangikaran" ("Making Education One's Own") read out in the 'Education Week' as an international 'New Education Fellowship' address on 8 February 1936 and published in the Visva-Bharati Bulletin on

20 Magh, 1342 Rabindranath expresses in an autobiographical vein that no one is sure that his mental maturity is the contribution of his unadulterated learning through the mother-tongue right from the early stage of his life. The sustenance he had received through it was so amply enriched that the Creator, he wondered, might touch the spell of magic in it. His sense of indebtedness to the mother-tongue that allows freedom of thought and expression in one's creative and critical sensibilities is adroitly expressed in the following words :

> From the very early childhood, my entry to the storehouse of the Bengali language was unbarred. Whatsoever meagre the components are there in that storehouse, it was sufficient for the maintenance and satisfaction of the mind of the child. The fasting mind has not to lose its breath and tread on by limping on the upward path of the foreign language. As there was no regular and serious head-on collision between learning and understanding, I was not brought up in the hospital of the school.
>
> There are other reasons for gratitude as well. The fundamental aspect of education is the pursuit to express in words the thoughts and ideas of the mind. It is the symptom of the healthy mind to make the very synchronization of this give-and-take process inwardly and outwardly. If the foreign language becomes the principal medium of cultivation of expression, it turns out as if like the habit of expression of ideas through the mask.
>
> —Rabindranath Tagore : "Sikshar Swangikaran", *Siksha*, Visva-Bharati, 1973, p. 242.
>
> [Translated by me]

In fact, demasking the medium of expression and freedom of spontaneity are the crying needs of education in the true sense of the term. When education wails in suppression of feelings and imagination, individuality suffers most, and when individuality is imprisoned civilization mocks at humanity.

IV. *Education for Aesthetic and Creative Development*

If education is eventually a realization of a being within

being, the unconditioned and the transcendent with its self-existent, unabridged freedom and delight that no other factor can so effectively and substantially contribute, it must be realized that the inner spirit of an individual can only be most successfully ignited through an exercise of his creative and aesthetic development. As a matter of fact, elimination of finer sense and sensibilities and softer emotions of life and lack of cultivation of mental faculty of imagination so peculiarly one's own have brought about a sort of social and national imbalance and incoherence. Good sense, alas, has already been questioned and good behaviour considered to be an alien matter in our day to day interaction. Consequently, with taming of technology and advancement of science, taming of human behaviour is yet a far cry. With no bond of union amongst persons, families, societies, communities and nations tearing off all finer traits of personality—love, compassion, integrity, modesty, co-operation—the mainstream of world communion is severely confronted with an unforeseen crisis—crisis of character leading to danger of extinction. Creativity, too, confused in the massacre of scientific and technological chivalries in the forms of automations and hi-tech caricature, aggression of electronics and flood and fury of gadgets, finds intoxicating happiness in illusory slumber. What a loss of human qualities!

Sharply reacting to all these, Rabindranath wants an uncompromising breakthrough, a radical switch-over from all kinds of passivities. Cultivation of the sense of goodness, adoration of the true, good and beautiful in one's life, preparation of a better life through observance of simple, unassuming, natural facts of life like decorating the house with flowers and foliages, boutique work, burning of incense, cleaning the surroundings, showing reverence to senior persons, serving the sick and the distressed persons, the old and the infirm, welcoming guests and strangers, speaking in a soft and sonorous, slow and sombre voice that appeals to one and all, loving neighbours and sharing their happiness and sufferings, lending a helping hand to the poor and the oppressed—all these, in brief, are some of the essential activities through which the aesthetic and creative sensibilities are manifested in a natural and lively atmosphere. Added to these are the all-endearing effects of performing arts *e.g.* dance, drama, music etc. that mould the passionate urge of humanity in an objective manner.

That education remains incomplete in the absence of exercise of aesthetics and creativity can hardly be denied. Rabindranath particularly emphasizes on this crucial and vital aspect of education and categorically states that even learning for living or learning for doing cannot ignore aesthetics and creativity. In fact, in his own school *Siksha-Satra* fondly christened by him as *The Poet's School*—a legend in the history of education for teaching aesthetics and creativity in an unambiguous and natural atmosphere, he wants all avenues wide open for efflorescence and emancipation of aesthetic and creative sensibilities. In his own words :

> The aim of *Siksha-Satra* is, through experience in dealing with the over-flowing abundance of child-life, its charm and simplicity, to provide the utmost liberty, within the surroundings that are filled with the creative possibilities with opportunities for the joy of play—the reaping of succession of novel experiences, to give the child freedom of growth which the young tree demands for its tender shoot, that field for self-expression in which all young life finds both training and experien ce.
>
> —*The Visva-Bharati Bulletin,* Visva-Bharati No. 9, 1928.

Today when education bids good-bye to joy and creativity and makes learners caged and cornered by leaving aside the natural atmosphere of abundance and originality, a look back and look within for revival of creative and aesthetic consciousness in the pursuit of knowledge is not only desirable but perhaps inevitable in order to effectively combat the rough challenges of life. In fact, work-education or work-experience so vigorously launched for the education of young learners is nothing but a sandwitched outcome of Tagore's educational experiments practised in his own school. *Siksha-Satra*.

It is interesting to note in this connection, L.K. Elmhirt's observations on the process of learning at *Siksha-Satra* :

> Records are kept and reports and accounts are written up,

revised and corrected giving scope for literary training in its most interesting form. Geology becomes the fertility of the plot; chemistry the use of lime and manures of all kinds of spray and disinfectants; physics the use of tools, pumps, the study of water-lift and oil engines; entomology the control of plant pests (ants, caterpillars, beetles) and diseases (leaf curl, wilt, bacterial attacks); orinthology, the study of birds in their relation first to the garden plot and to the world in general.

There is no room in Siksha-Satra for Nature-study as an abstract subject, diversed from life and needs of life.**

**In life the child has to face the mosquito mightily, perhaps the bug, or flea, the bacterial of ptyphoid, of cholera, of small-pox as well as the forces of nature which attack his trees, his plants and his livestock. Nature-study is thus transferred into the study of nature in relation to life and daily experiences of life.

—L.K. Elmhirst : *Rabindranath Tagore : Pioneer in Education*, John Murry, London, 1961, pp. 73-74.

With so much know-how and so little know-why as modern educational experiments and innovations bear forth, the creative urge that pulsates the joy of living together can save, and save alone, humanity split in innumerable fragments. The conversations matter of fact and stale, the mutual relations torn and tattered, love and sympathy bored and banished—all culminate to the sense of hollowness of life lost in bare living. As Tagore observes, human reality is being killed everywhere by the imposition of the abstract to arrest creativity and consciousness. Thus the slaughter of subjectivity so ghastly committed in our modern educational programmes that chivalroustly chalk out production-oriented schemes and programmes for development necessitates a nemesis. The denouement is already performed. Who comes save Rabindranath, for regeneration of human creativity ?

The *Ashramic* education that Tagore so seriously wanted to introduce proclaims the spirit of creativity, the worship of the inherent 'I' that yet bewails in Websterian wailing as voiced forth in his drama *The Duchess of Malfi* : 'O life, no life, but lovely remains of death'. The relation between the teacher and the taught is based on the pre-supposition that there must be a creative and dynamic interchange of ideas and thoughts, of experiences and innovations, of facts and imagination. This, as Rabindranath categorically assets, is a sort of meditation—*sadhana*—as he states in his essay *Ashramer Siksha,* the education of the Ashrama. When there is a union of minds, the joy in creativity emanates—the joy that is nothing but the contribution of oneness—where the teacher and the taught mingle in the great ocean of erudition in an untiring endeavour to delve deep and find out and feel the vista of enlightenment, the spirit eternal. As an exponent of this spirit eternal, Rabindranath highlights the sense of curiosity very poignantly :

> It is absence of curiosity that indicates the passivity of the mind. Today the nations dominating over the world have exhibited their indomitable curiosity upon everything of this world. There is neither any country nor any time nor, again, any subject towards which their mind is not being thrust forward. This living power of mind on their part came out victorious throughout the world.
>
> ***The education of the Ashram is to live in fulness. One can ascend the highest peak of the first class in the examination even with a dead mind. We are regularly accustomed to this fact in our country. It is seen that the very good students of the college secure titles of honour but never secure the world. From the very beginning, I had the resolution that the boys of the Ashram would remain curious of having immediate relations all around. They will seek, examine and collect. Here teachers whose visions spread beyond the horizon of books would assemble.
>
> —Rabindranath Tagore : "Ashramer Siksha", *Siksha,* Visva-Bharati 1973, pp. 248-49.
>
> [Translated by me]

Fulness in education welcomes fulness of human creativity wedded to curiosity. Education for the premotion of such kind of individuality broadens the vision of human consciousness to explore newer possibilities of mankind and worthier advancements of human civilization. The education for creative and aesthetic development, as Tagore believes and shows in practice of performance, enhances civilization a great deal.

V. *Education for Social Awareness and National Integration*

Education for social awareness and national integration is in essence the education for human relationship. Tagore takes it a challenge for introducing a new system of mass education to avert the curse of the bondage of the human mind. Apathy and ignorance are, as he wants to hammer on the conscience of humanity, the worst forms of bondage. Humanity must be made free from this bondage. To attack and arrest ignorance, he does not blame the yoked condition of a future-blurred politically conscious India, nor does he give importance to national independence over and above national crisis—consciousness-crisis or rather that of education.

Very often misunderstood and erroneously enlisted in the melee of the world of the elite. Tagore has the endearing heart to feel the pulse of the poor and the distressed whose life-blood has strengthened the stream of livelihood of the so-called intellectual urbanites. Fashioned in furores and popular with agitations and sentimental revolutions, the so-called national reformers hardly reacted to the will of the masses intrinsically and understood their inner urge to unmask ignorance and welcome education. Instead, the Curzonian downward filtration theory even now, alas, ironically back-clapped and supported in our failure to introduce primary education free, universal and compulsory and warming up higher education with mushroom growth of universities everywhere and anywhere at the invaluable cost of public money engulfs the entire programmes for education in our country. Side by side with this, the woes of the ordinary men and women of our country are aggravated because the rate of illiteracy and the deplorable condition of andragogy ever afraid of paper tigers and contented with casual learnings to be either stagnated or stopped out with reshuffling of political portfolios are yet beyond care and care.

Dissatisfied with this imperialistic, commercial, parochial, patchwork type of education, Rabindranath introduces a new system of education that is rooted to the soil of the country and the world in the broad sense of the term. He gives stress on *Yatra*, *Kathakata*, the songs of the *Ramayana*, the *Kavigaan* and shows the avenue of reviving the spirit of rural unity. Moreover, with emphasis on learning through the mother-tongue which he considers to be equivalent to the breast milk of the mother, he opens out a new hope of regeneration of social and creative awareness. Unlike traditional reformers normally harping on the Western ideas of educational experimentations, Tagore himself breaks a new ground by introducing *Lok-Siksha Samsad* (People's Education Council) for advancement of education of the adults and the deprived. Even in his own *The Poet's School*, experiments on education through imparting practical assignments for boys and girls coming from near-by rural areas, working all day long—sowing seeds, planting saplings, seedlings, plants etc., weaving clothes, using tools and indigenous gadgets, ploughing fields, washing utensils, cleaning rooms and adjoining areas and executing manifold activities of head and heart—pave newer avenues of the joy of learning by doing and learning by living. Self-reliance and self-activity are the two very important weapons that Rabindranath wonderfully introduces through the Department of Rural Extension of the Institution of Rural Reconstruction of Sriniketan. Occasional checks through analysis and evaluation of activities pertaining to social advancements by means of social and cultural activities sponsored by the said institute mark a new dimension of Tagore as a social thinker.

Again, the sense of unity and harmony so gradually decreasing in a world of seek, hurry and divided aims has been serenely and adroitly introduced for the first time in our country when Rabindranath christens the economically and socially ruined rural people with the spirit of co-operative endeavour. Being bewildered in poverty and shrouded in the ignorance of mischief that is also untimely afoot with dwindling economy, village people even now fall a hapless prey to the aggravating money-lenders. With the introduction of co-operative banks by Tagore, a new lease of life among rural people has ushered forth. Moreover, the concept of thrift has been successfully introduced among school children to lay by something even when they are prosecuting their studies.

Rabindranath as a social connoisseur has for the first time shown that with advancement of education throughout the country, communal tensions and disruptive tendencies can be effectively done away with very quickly. With the introduction of his unparalleled *Rakhi Vandhan Utsav* (Safety and Integration Ceremony), an integral part of education even now observed in his own educational institutions at Santiniketan and Sriniketan, violence and communalism can be smoothly rooted out. Who denies this splendid avenue of eradicating social ills like communalism, violence, hatred, corruption etc. at a crucial time when we look askance at one another very shrewdly and critically and breathe a heavy air of passivity, uneasiness and hopelessness? To be socially useful and aware of the needs of others we are badly in need of that type of education that elevates us from being a man to *men* by means of education as desired by Rabindranath. Have we really responded to his intentions ?

POINTS TO PONDER

From a study of the aforesaid essence of Tagore's educational thoughts and experiments some of which are even now practised in his own Visva-Bharati in right earnest, the following might be considered for educational re-orientation :

(i) The role of the mother-tongue for a pupil's natural growth and development as a learner should be more specifically emphasized and education right from the primary upto the highest level be introduced, enriched and evaluated by means of the mother-tongue. Serious thinking should also be geared to the introduction of the mother-tongue in all possible academic and administrative machineries so that alien learning matters and components may be switched over to the mother-tongue within a very short time. A wider avenue of consciousness for large-scale use of the mother-tongue would fillip a new aura of advancement in the continental system of education.

(ii) For furtherance of educational advancement, the role of environment as Tagore emphasizes should claim serious re-thinking. To be attuned with Nature is to be blessed with the blessings of the best teacher. To be attuned with Nature, again, and the surroundings as a homogeneous set of unit is not merely to adorn Nature but to be vitalized in the most pulsating manner, and education through Nature implies one that paves path to the desirable goal of fulness. The crisis of character, loss of moral values, ethical erosions, absence of finer sense and sensibilities, erosion of simplicity and modest way of leading one's life—all rooted to the soil of our indigenous system of education so ruthlessly replaced by the alien ones—can only be averted through the *Tapovan* system of education as introduced by Tagore in Santiniketan with minor modifications, if necessary. Who averts the truth so relevant from time immemorial as revealed in the words of Wordsworth?

One impulse from a vernal wood
May teach you more of man
Of moral evil and of good
Than all the sages can.

—William Wordsworth : "The Tables Turned". *Poetry and Prose*, O.U.P.

(iii) Side by side with the incorporation of aesthetic education as referred to earlier by decorating the floors with *alpanas*, walls with paintings externally and internally, and with the exercise of mental imagination and creativity in dealing with manifold personalities intrinsically, the holding of functions and festivals in line with global culture and tradition would not only boost the sense of social and global harmony but would also enable everyone to be initiated with the true religion of man.

(iv) Though incorporation of adult education in the regular system of education in accordance with the ideas of Rabindranath, the problem of eradication of mass illiteracy and ignorance may be more effectively tackled than by the National Service Scheme which is more a ritual than the service proper. In addition to this, the system of holding the *Ananda Bazar Utsav*, an annual pre-autumn recess festival organized by the students themselves at Santiniketan, in which pupils exhibit and sell their self-manufactured products bearing prominence of their creative and aesthetic genius, and contribute the entire sale-proceeds to the Students' Aid Fund, is yet a rare and emulating example for every educational institution for a real awakening of social and global consciousness.

(v) Revival of the basic needs of performing arts like dance, drama, music etc. as emphasized and introduced by Tagore at Visva-Bharati is not only a pointer to enrichment of culture but the same also enables every human being to realize the inner worth to be alive with the ideas of what is true, good and beautiful to one and all. This also stimulates synchronization of the individual and the social self so dissociated in cultural bankruptcy and so ignored in, for example, our national system of education that is rest assured with exhibitionism in futile youth hostels and youth festivals.

(vi) Introduction of self-discipline and self-education by means of launching programmes like *Brati-Balak* Organisation as Tagore thinks for young boys may also be considered for fulness in education.

(vii) The programme of teacher education in the light of Tagore's concept of the role of the teacher in an emerging world might be re-evaluated. In this connection, the following invaluable words of Tagore might assure re-thinking with firm promises to be carried out in our educational plans and programmes about the role of the teacher :

> Education seems to me essentially an art, whose problem we solve not by discussing systems but by

discovering creative sources of inspiration. When the source is a human one he resides in a teacher who is a student and through whom a perennial intellectual eagerness as a dynamic force spreads in its surroundings a disinterested impulse for knowledge. * * * The teachers should be ideal comrades of those whom they teach, and through the course of teaching their own minds should be stirred in sympathy with the string of young minds. The joy of imbibing lessons oneself ought to find its true expression infusing in others.

—Rabindranath Tagore : "Message to New Education Fellowship Conference", *The Modern Review*, Calcutta, 1937.

(viii) For a brighter prospect of humanity and, for that end in view, human civilization, the education for universal brotherhood of mankind necessitates re-thinking from the Tagorean perspectives. As he often reminds the horror-stricken people of the world, empathy and not apathy is the only way of averting the crisis—the crisis of civilization. As hatred begets hatred, the re-birth of compassion is not only what should be the prayer of mankind but a practice in performance in right earnest also. Today's world awaits more *Rishis* in practical educational endeavour than spiritual accomplishments howsoever desirable and worthwhile.

(ix) The harmony of human consciousness as Tagore seeks in the pursuit of education for fulness is, indeed, the harmony of human endeavour. The cross fertilization of culture, an incomparable and poignant expression which is the core of education is what Tagore suggests as an antidote to every type of human disintegration and disbelief. As he remained faithful to the unending possibilities of human endeavour and considered the loss of faith in man to be a great sin, why not pin ardent hopes on the education for mutual belief and sympathy ?

WHY NOT *METANOIA* ?

It is high time that in our system of education the curriculum at every level should act as a spurt to manifest the intrinsic value of humanity. A curriculum is more than a taxonomy of topics and concepts. Its multi-dimensional approach as Tagore so characteristically implemented in his own educational institutions in the development of skills, attitudes, interests, appreciation, awareness of values and creative and aesthetic potentialities can hardly be bogged down as mere offshoots of sentimentalism but should be idealised and imbibed for the victory of man as man. Who denies that ours is a country of spontaneity particularly in the arena of creativity and the eternal heritage of civilizatlon has its origin in the land of our birth in many respects ? Meanwhile, the world of education is preparing for an outright change. Why not re-orient ourselves for judicious protest against merciless slaughters of subjectivity and enter into the world of *metanoia* for the true recognition of man as man ?

THE MYSTIC MUSE IN *SONG OFFERINGS*

A whole people, a whole civilization, a whole universe in wonder and askance, joy and love, sorrow and pain, delight and mystery or in union and separation eternally muse on. Who harps on that muse out of his own abundant experience of life beyond life ? Who translates the words of the mind for a prized beyonding of consciousness ? Who turns poetry into the language of the soul beyond soul ? All these and a host of other queries place us nearer to Rabindranath Tagore to inhale the mystic perfume of promise for greater advancement of mankind sordid in pains and happy in happiness but on the whole continually contented in Miltonian 'calmness of mind all passions spent.' An entry into the mystic muse in *Song Offerings* leads the mind in quest of infinite possibilities of experiencing the thrilling voice of a poet who defies the transcient objects of Nature to welcome and endear her poignance in affluence in human life and this is evident in manifold patterns of mystic subtleties almost everywhere in Tagore's *Song Offerings.* As W.B. Yeats observes,

> A whole people, a whole civilization, immeasurably strange to us, seems to have been taken up into this imagination; and yet we are not moved because of its strangeness, but because we have met our own image, as though we had walked in Rossett's willow wood, or heard, perhaps for the first time in literature, our voice as in a dream.
>
> —W.B. Yeats : "Introduction", *Song Offerings,* Macmillan Pocket Tagore Edition, Macmillan India Limited, 1981, pp. xiii-xiv.

Profoundly soaked in the poignance of humility, the Poet

takes an account of himself—a sort of self-assessment—that marks the preparation of his inward vision ?

> The song that I came to sing remains unsung to this day.
> I have spent my days in stringing and in unstringing my instrument.
> The time has not come true, the words have not been rightly set; only there is the agony of wishing in my heart.
>
> —*Song Offerings*, XIII

To wait for the blossoming of life is to wait for the message to be brought forth by the 'sighing wind'. The Poet has this agony of the soul to welcome the Ever Beautiful. The preparation with the muse eternal goes on for the long awaited welcome : a well spread out floor *sans* the bright lamp to great the All Endearing poses before him a sense of uncertainty. Will all his muse end in smoke ?

> I have not seen his face, nor have I listened to his voice; only I have heard his gentle footsteps from the road before my house.
> The livelong day has passed in spreading his seat on the floor; but the lamp has not been lit and I cannot ask him into my house.
> I live in the hope of meeting with him; but this meeting is not yet.
>
> —*Song Offerings*, XIII

With the waning of each day, the Poet feels a sense of desolation, since the languid days of his life has made the vision of the All Beautiful utterly blurred. He feels that he has been cruelly averted :

> There are times when I languidly linger and times when I awaken and hurry in search of my goal; but cruelly thou hidest thyself from me.
>
> —*Song Offerings*-XIV

Does the Poet feel frustrated for the refusal ? He is ready to find out his answer in the muse :

> Day by day thou art making me worthy of thy full

acceptance by refusing me ever and anon, saving me from perils of weak, uncertain desire.

—*Song Offerings*, XIV

Already, the Poet is assured within himself that he is blessed with the 'strong mercy' of the All Beautiful who always saves him from his 'overmuch desire' only to be worthy of the 'great gifts'—the body, the mind, the life, the light, the sky—in and around him :

My desires are many and my cry is pitiful, but ever didst thou save me by hard refusals; and this strong mercy has been wrought into my life through and through.

Day by day thou art making me worthy of the simple, great gifts that thou gavest to me unasked—this sky and the light, this body and the life and the mind—saving me from perils of overmuch desire.

—*Song Offerings*, XIV

With benign adoration spreading wings 'like a glad bird on its flight across the sea', the Poet waits for the command of the Life of his life to sing with a pride that presents him with tears of gratitude. The hemlock of joy that he derives out of his mystic muse eliminates all differences, all distance between him and the Lord and he greets the latter as his friend to sing together endlessly.

Does he come upto the cadence of his Friend's song ? The Poet thinks and thinks. In 'silent amazement' he listens and in humble adoration he elucidates the mystic resonance of his experience :

The light of thy mystic illumines the world. The life breadth of thy music runs from sky to sky. The holy stream of thy music breaks through all stony obstacles and rushes on.

My heart longs to join in thy song, but vainly struggles for a voice. I would speak, but speech breaks not into song, and I cry out baffled. Ah, thou hast made my heart captive in the endless meshes of thy music, my master !

—*Song Offerings*, III

The rainbow of the Friend's song spreads dreams in multitudinous colour and splendour and the Poet knows not how to appreciate. His language soaks in tears, his voice choaks in the aroma of mystic beauty wherein his ideas and expressions are garbed in silence.

The 'living touch' of the Life of his life brings forth the mystic oath for the Poet :

> I shall ever try to keep my body pure, knowing that thy living touch is upon all my limbs.
>
> —*Song Offerings*, IV

Furthermore, he has other oaths to be renewed with infinite source of inspiration that he desires from the 'Life of his life' :

> I shall ever try to keep all untruths out from my thoughts, knowing that thou art that truth which has kindled the light of reason in my mind.
>
> I shall ever try to drive all evils away from my heart and keep my love in flower knowing that thou hast thy seat in the inmost shrine of my heart.
>
> And it shall be my endeavour to reveal thee in my actions, knowing it is thy power gives me strength to act.
>
> —*Song Offerings*, IV

From all imperfections and inabilities, the Poet is fired with the spirit of the mystic promise—'the promise of a golden harvest' because he believes that the mystic light that illumines his inner vision will bring forth the fruits of his lost world of consciousness, his lost kingdom of being.

Perhaps, the Poet has already prepared himself with the truth that not salvation but the very spirit of renunciation through purity of perfection will show him the gateway to the Heaven of the great Illuminator.

How to reveal the 'imprisoned splendour' ? Sleepless like a seasoned mystic, the Poet is restless. The long awaited stormy night has at last come. The meeting with the All Beautiful is just to take place. Does He appear with all constraints in the form of the groaning Nature ?

I have no sleep tonight. Ever and again I open my door and look out on the darkness, my friend!

I can see nothing before me. I wonder where lies thy path!

By what dim shore of the ink-black river, by what far edge of the frowning forest, through what mazy depth of gloom art thou threading thy course to come to me, my friend?

—*Song Offerings*, XXIII

A sudden call to apparently useless consequence as the Poet looks at men hurrying to the King's market makes him prepared for a prayer in mystic fulness. The cathersis of life tolls for the time and the Poet is prepared to endear his great Friend with all his emptiness beyond 'the strife of the good and the evil'. As he frankly proclaims :

No more noisy, loud words from me—such is my master's will. Henceforth I deal in whispers. The speech of my heart will be carried on in murmurings of a song.

Men hasten to the King's market. All the buyers and sellers are there. But I have my untimely leave in the middle of the day, in the thick of work.

—*Song Offerings*, LXXXIX

With this resolution for premature farewell as he feels mystically within himself, the Poet has a benign appeal for the noontime bees to come in the garden of his life at such untimely lazy hours :

Let then the flowers come out in my garden, though it is not their time; and let the midday bees strike up their lazy hum.

—*Song Offerings*, LXXXIX

And with the humming of the lazy bees, the Poet looks forward for the mystic pleasure of the empty days :

Full many an hour have I spent in the strife of the good and the evil, but now it is the pleasure of my playmate of

> the empty days to draw my heart on to him; and I know not why is this sudden call to what useless inconsequence !
>
> —*Song Offerings*, LXXXIX

How does the Poet adorn himself with the mystic light ? How does he enter into the Kingdom of light beyond light ? How does he prepare himself for a grand entry into the King's palace ? All these are woven in magnificent flowers of words in his Song Offerings, placed at the altar of the All Beautiful.

A saner, simpler pattern of mysticism synchronized with the day to day affairs of life makes the Poet our very own. Or is he pointing towards the Sufi truth of the real nature of a mystic that everyone has a *Darvish* in his soul ? The mingling of light in diverse moments of life is the very mingling of the vision of a great mystic visionary playing with life and the different ways and experiences of life with great contentment. Aren't all great poets fundamentally great mystics ?

The light that dawns on in the inward heartland of the Poet makes him eager for a vision of the King of his heart in silence. Even the clamour of the wind might break the silence and serenity of atmosphere amid the mystic sleep of grandeur in the morning festival of light.

> If the sound of his steps does not wake me, do not try to rouse me. I pray. I wish not to be called from my sleep by the clamorous choir of birds, by the riot of wind at the festival of morning light.
>
> —*Song Offerings*, XLVII

How does the Poet yearn for the King's arrival ? How would he celebrate his return to himself ? He has an humble appeal :

> Let him appear before my sight as the first of all lights and all forms. The first thrill of joy to my awakened soul let it come from his glance. And let my return to myself be immediate return to him.
>
> —*Song Offerings*, XLVII

In the festival light the inward world of the Poet flashes with the blessings of the King in the form of Truth eternal.

He feels that all his sense and sensibilities, power of reasonings and erudition is hallowed with the radiance of light as a gift from his king. The living touch he receives from Him prepares him for swearing an oath in the mystic vein :

> I shall ever try to keep all untruths out from my thoughts, knowing that thou art that truth which has kindled the light of reason in my mind.
>
> —*Song Offerings*, IV

The Poet feels within himself the agony of the not-yet, the *adhara* and the burning desires, 'false and empty to the core', as he introspects, await the fruits of his frantic appeal for the light in 'I want thee, only thee' :

> As the night keeps hidden its gloom the petition for light, even thus in the depth of my consciousness rings the cry—'I want thee, only thee'.
>
> As the storm still seeks its end in peace when it strikes against peace with all its might, even thus my rebellion strikes against thy love and still its cry is—'I want thee, only thee'.
>
> —*Song Offerings*, XXXVIII

When does the Poet want to meet his King, his 'lord of silence' ? He waits for the mystic moments and these moments are purified and bathed in his delusion and dust in blind desires. He wants the climax of 'tumultuous work' that raises the din of clamour and makes him restless only to present him with the 'peace and rest' of the Ever Wakeful :

> When tumultuous work raises its din on all sides shutting me out from beyond, come to me, my lord of silence, with thy peace and rest.
>
> When my beggarly heart sits crouched, shut up in a corner, break open the door, my king, and come with the ceremony of a King.
>
> When desire blinds the mind with delusion and dust, O thou holy one, thou wakeful, come with thy light and thy thunder.
>
> —*Song Offerings*, XXXIX

For the festival of light—the light of mystic serenity—the Poet is fully prepared to greet the King of kings in 'golden splendour' :

> I sit on the grass and gaze upon the sky and dream of the sudden splendour of thy coming—all the lights ablaze, golden pennons flying over thy car, and they at the road-side standing agape, when they see thee come down from thy seat to raise me from the dust, and set at thy side this ragged beggar girl a-tremble with shame and pride, like a creeper in a summer breeze.
>
> —*Song Offerings*, XLI

Does this futility in him make him rather a prey to desolation ? Is his mystic belief in the Eternal Illuminator shattered in shambles of hopelessness ? Let us hear the Poet's muse :

> I know not how thou singest, my master !
> I ever listen in silent amazement.
>
> The light of thy music illumines the world. The life breath of thy music runs from sky to sky. The holy stream of thy music breaks through all stony obstacles and rushes on.
>
> —*Song Offerings*, III

A 'captive in the endless meshes' of the music of the master, the Poet knows it very well that to find delight in the desires of the waiting heart alone in the magnificent panorama of Nature is to breathe an air of consolation because the message of the mystic unknown is the message of gladness within the mind :

> This is my delight, thus to wait and watch at the wayside where shadow chases light and the rain comes in the wake of the summer.
>
> Messengers, with tidings from unknown skies, greet me and speed along the road. My heart is glad within, and the breath of the passing breeze is sweet.
>
> —*Song Offerings*, XLIV

The 'tidings from unknown' spheres make the Poet restless for the *adhara*, the not-yet, and he is now in the mood of a child to be lost anywhere in the freedom of thought and inner intentions, he waits for the laurels of despair and defeat, while all honour awaits 'the heroic host' :

> All honour to you, heroic host of the interminable path ! Mockery and reproach pricked me to rise, but found no response in me. I gave myself up for lost in the depth of a glad humiliation—in the shadow of a dim delight.
>
> —*Song Offerings*, XLVIII

Amid despair and desolation that make the Poet self-forgetful and serene with a begging bowl to meet the King of all kings, the splendour of the golden light suddenly flashes on the chariot in the distance and the moment of wonder springs in his mind :

> I had gone a-begging from door to door in the village path, when thy golden chariot appeared in the distance like a gorgeous dream and I wondered who was this King of all kings !
>
> —*Song Offerings*, L

The mystic moment, indeed, comes when the King of all kings alights from his golden chariot, stands before the Poet and asks for the offerings. What, as a beggar, does he offer to be returned to the King ? It is the grandeur of 'the gorgeous dream' that awaits him to see the kingly jest ? Is the return of 'the least little grain of corn' by the King in the form of 'a least little gram of gold' the mystic finale for him to be purified in the incessant shedding of tears ?

> Ah, what a kingly jest was it to open thy palm to a beggar to beg ! I was confused and stood undecided, and then from my wallet I slowly took out the least little grain of corn to give it to thee.
>
> But how great my surprise when at the day's end I emptied bag on the floor to find a least little gram of gold among the poor heap. I bitterly wept and wished that I had had the heart to give thee my all.
>
> —*Song Offerings*, L

The pressing of this signet for mystic eternity by the Lord of silence makes the Poet conscious of the sailing in a boat, a joint pilgrimage, to the mystic unknown. The wavelike free muse of the Poet is a sombre revelation of the great journey ahead into eternity amidst the mystic aroma of darkness :

> In that shoreless ocean, at the silently listening smile my songs would swell in melodies, free as waves, free from all bondage of words.
>
> Is the time not come yet ? Are these works still to do ? Lo, the evening has come down upon the shore and in the fading light the sea birds come flying to their nests.
>
> Who knows when the chains will be off, and the boat, like the last glimmer of sunset, vanish into the night ?
>
> *Song Offerings*, XLII

The same mystic vision of darkness appears in the Poet's autobiographical vein in the form of a poem in the description of his 'fancies' elsewhere :

> My fancies are fireflies
> Specks of living light—twinkling in the dark
>
> —"*Lekhan*", *Rabindra-Rachanavali*, Volume II, Poems, Collected Works of Rabindranath Tagore (1861-1941), Government of West Bengal, Calcutta, 1982, p. 723
>
> [Translated by me]

For the sweet music of pain arising from the inmost depth of his heart, the Poet feels a mystic splendour of light—the light that never fails to show the avenues of love, beauty, affluence of joy and gladness. Is this light the presence of the mystic *Paransakha* symbolizlng the Poet's love in profusion for the beloved of his heart of hearts ?

> Light, my light, the world-filling light, the eye-kissing light, heart-sweetening light !
>
> Ah, the light dances, my darling, at the centre of my life; the light strikes, my darling, the chords of my love; the sky opens, the wind runs wild, laughter passes over the earth.
>
> The butterflies spread their sails on the sea of light. Lilies and jasmines surge up on the crest of the waves of light.

The light is shattered into gold on every cloud, my darling, and it scatters gems in profusion.

Mirth spreads from leaf to leaf, my darling, and gladness without measure. The heaven's river has drowned its banks and the flood of joy is abroad.

Song Offerings, LVII

The same yearning for light in the backdrop of wild wind and black night is revealed when the Poet appeals to the Lord at the mystic moment's flash of lightning :

Light, oh where is the light ! Kindle it with the burning fire of desire ! It thunders and the wind rushes screaming through the void. The night is black as a black stone. Let not the hours pass by in the dark.

Song Offerings, XXVII

The blessings of defeat that 'come in the life of the Poet in the form of darkness make the Poet a great mystic in the muse of self-submission. That the defeat he meets is the preparation for reunion with the Lord forms the foundation of the modest language of his muse :

Then take away your hands and silently put up with your defeat, my heart, and think it your good fortune to sit perfectly still where you are placed.

These my lamps are blown out at every little puff of wind, and trying to light them I forget all else again and again.

But I shall be wise this time and wait in the dark, spreading my mat on the floor, and whenever it is thy pleasure, my lord, come silently and take thy seat here.

Song Offerings, XCIX

Like Milton who hails holy light as the offspring of heaven, Tagore considers light as the mystic shadow of the Lord. As the Lord Himself is light—'the light of death', as the Poet introspectively feels—let the last farewell be a beyonding from all barriers of time. As he muses on :

I know that the day will come when my sight of this earth shall be lost, and life will take its leave in silence, drawing the last curtain over my eyes.

Yet stars will watch as night, and morning rise as before, and hours heave like sea waves casting like pleasures and pain.

When I think of this end of my moments, the barrier of the moments breaks and I see by the light of death thy world with its careless treasures.

—*Song Offerings*, XCII

The mystic panorama of light and the Poet's vision of union with the Endless create an indescribable atmosphere of awe and wonder throughout *Song Offerings*. Like a great saint he controls his passion in an absolutely vacant mood of self-submission and self-forgetfulness. The light of the Lord that he receives enriches his inward vision and awaits re-birth in *Karuna* or compassion of the All Compassionate.

Secondly, the light of the King appears to the Poet as the symbol of emancipation from all petty ignorance. It stands for the mystic revelation of consciousness for truth. He muses with great mystic contentment :

***thou art that truth which has enkindled the light of reason in my mind.

Song Offerings, IV

Thirdly, as the Poet believes in the mystic truth that the Light of the Lord encompasses the mind, the light of His music illumines the world. It is the light that leads the mind from the darkness of ignorance to the light of heavenly music.

With this mystic belief in the infinite power of the Light of the Lord, the Poet enjoys the mystic atmosphere of Nature—her abundance of infinite beauty in the morning and the evening, her silence like a sombre saint, her vastness like a sea, her emptiness like the endless sea-shore, her promises like 'the first gleam of light' and her poignance like sorrow, pain, pleasure, austerity and nothingness, futility and fulness. The mystic symbols that associate with such a serene atmosphere are the earth and the sky, the sea and the sea-birds, the mother and the child. the lover and the Lord Himself. Added to all these are the sun, the moon, the stars, the garlands, the flute, the travaller and the beggar appearing as mystic replicas of the body and the mind and the life enriched in imageries and imaginations.

With varied experiences to agonies and anxieties that penetrated the Poet's soft sensibilities throughout the life, the mystic muse in *Song Offerings* presents us with an altogether new dimension of mystic tranquillity. The Eternal Lord of Beauty, as the Poet visualizes in his depth of vision, appears before us in the mystic imagery of flowers and breaks forth in the fountain of music :

> **thy melodies will break forth in flowers.
>
> —*Song Offerings* XIX

Even if the flowers are withered and dead, futile and useless representing decadence symbolically, the Poet does not avert the new lease of life with the optimistic note of the advent of the spring, the mystic rebirth of beauty :

> The spring has done its flowering and taken leave. And now with the burden of faded futile flowers I wait and linger.
>
> —*Song Offerings*, XXI

When does the Poet 'wait and linger' ? He mystically suggests the answer with a bold and optimistic promise in his muse :

> I must launch out my boat.
>
> —*Song Offerings*, XXI

For the mystic renewal of consciousness, the Poet takes the role of a traveller in search of beyondings and the symbol of a flower for his life plays on in his song in sonorous music :

> From the traveller, whose sack of provisions is empty before the voyage is ended, whose garment is torn and dustladen, whose strength is exhausted, remove shame and poverty, and renew his life like a flower under the cover of the kindly night.
>
> —*Song Offerings*, XXIV

It is interesting to note that the Poet wants to endear the endless mytery of night that he thinks so kind as to allow him to have his renewal of consciousness in the mystic beauty of the night. The veil of night drawn by the Lord is, as he strongly believes in his mystic temperament. a pulsating promise for 'a fresher gladness of awakening'.

The 'dowry of poverty' consequential to the loss of all flowers forcibly taken away by passers-by is the Poet's pride in affluence of nothingness. And this pride, as he also thinks is the 'secret' of his heart. Like Milton proclaiming the mystic truth—'They also serve who only stand and wait' ("On his blindness")—Tagore also arrives at the point of mystic loneliness in, of coutse, a different pattern through humble submission in askance with a wearisome heart bereft of the flowers for offerings :

> But time glides on and still no sound of the wheels of thy chariot. Many a procession passes by with noise and shouts and glamour of glory. Is it only thou who wouldst stand in the shadow silent and behind them all ? And only I who would wait and weep and wear out my heart in vain longing ?
>
> —*Song Offerings*, XLI

The poignance in askance that the Poet makes 'in vain longing' also brings forth a mystic promise in his muse to meet his 'Life of my life' :

> I shall ever try to drive all evils away from heart and keep my love in flower, knowing that thou hast thy seat in the inmost shrine of my heart.
>
> —*Song Offerings*, IV

To sit face to face with the Lord of love and to sing the mystic muse of life necessitate an atmosphere of serene silence for the Poet who awaits the summer, the season of fulfilment of the longings of the thirsty heart pining for the sweet music of bees in the flowering grove. Here is the dramatic atmosphere painted in the mystic words of muse :

> Away from the sight of thy face my heart knows no rest

> nor respite, and my work becomes an endless toil in a shoreless sea of toil.
>
> Today the summer has come at my window with its sighs and murmurs; and the bees are plying their minstrelsy at the court of the flowering grove.
>
> Now it is time to sit quiet, face to face with thee, and to sing dedication of life in this silent and overflowing leisure.
>
> —*Song Offerings*, V

Does the Poet want to avert disappointment and endear silence ? What does he expect from his King ? The prize in the form of a flower from the Master—a flower of eternal glory of purity—is the reward of all rewards for him. The 'simple carol' becomes majestic with the magnanimous prize in the form of a flower from the hands of the King at the cottage door :

> Masters are many in your hall, and songs are sung there at all hours. But the simple carol of this novice struck at your love. One plaintive little strain mingled with the great music at the world, and with a flower for a prize you came down and stopped at my cottage door.
>
> —*Song Offerings*, XLVII

Occasionally, the Poet has a mystic faith on idle days in submitting himself to the Lord of creation. A sense of desolation engulfs his whole imagination. Being tired and exhausted, he seeks consolation in the inward vision of the Lord and the mystic 'wonder of flowers' adorns the garden of his life and mind :

> I was tired and sleeping on my idle bed and imagined all work had ceased. In the morning I woke up and found my garden full with wonders of flowers.
>
> —*Song Offerings*, LXXXI

The dancing of the stream of life, the coiling strength—*Kundalini Sakti*—rippling in the veins of the Poet brings forth the living faith in flowers and leaves in the mystic movement of endless waves. It is this dancing that makes him dynamic with the sense of freshness and beauty represented through leaves and flowers. As he muses :

> It is the same life that shoots in joy through the dust of the earth in numberless blades of grass and breaks into tumultuous waves of leaves and flowers.
>
> —*Song Offerings*, LXIX

The mystic sense of simplicity and innocence as the Poet represents through the saintly purity of children playing on the seashore of life marks a new epoch in the history of mysticism. The background is superbly drawn : the endless words of the motionless infinite sky, the boisterous ripples of restless water, sand houses, empty shells, withered leaves, 'pale gleams of the smile of the the sea beach' playing with the children like the mother's smiling care, the eternal play of death in the 'trackless water' of the sea—all create in unison a sense of unending mystery in the vast expanse of awe and wonder. The whole serene atmosphere of mystery spread through the magic web of words in a picturesque setting of children playing eternally on the sea-shore makes a thrilling sensation of sombre music :

> On the seashore of endless worlds children meet. The infinite sky is motionless overhead and the restless water is boisterous. On the seashore of endless worlds the children meet with shouts and dances.
>
> They build their houses with sand and they play with empty shells. With withered leaves they weave their boats and smilingly float them on the vast deep. Children have their play on the seashore of worlds.
>
> They know not how to swim, they know not how to cast nets. Pearl fishers dive for pearls, merchants sail in their ships, while children gather pebbles and scatter them again. They seek not for hidden treasures, they know not how to cast nets.
>
> The sea surges up with laughter and pale gleams the

smile of the sea beach. Death-dealing waves sing meaningless ballads to the children, even like a mother while rocking her baby's cradle. The sea plays with children, and pale gleams the smile of the sea beach.

On the sea shore of endless worlds children meet. Tempest roams in the pathless sky, ships get wrecked in the trackless water, death is abroad and children play. On the seashore of endless worlds is the great meeting of children.

Song Offerings, LX

The innocent play of the children in the weaving of their boats with 'withered leaves' for the endlsss sailing in the vast deep sea, the ignorance of how to swim or cast nets and how to seek the hidden treasures of the sea unlike pearl fishers and merchants and the meaningless ballads of the death-dealing waves adorn children with the saintly personality of poignance and simplicity. The imagery of the turbulent sea and the natural calmness of children shouting and dancing unendingly haunt the mind with a touchy reminiscence of childhood in the heavenly meeting of all children of the all Beautiful.

The Poet sincerely desires to allow this spontaneity of the child to play as and when he likes under natural settings. The blessings of mystic innocence and simplicity should not be tarnished with artificialities :

The child who is decked with prince's robes and who has jewelled chains round his neck loses all pleasure in his play; his dress hampers him at every step.

In fear that it may be frayed, or stained with dust he keeps himself from the world, and is afraid even to move.

—*Song Offerings*, VIII

Intensely endearing as the child is to the Poet, the mystery of his eyes, that of the smile in his lips or the 'soft freshness that blooms' on his limbs finds a mystic explanation in the alchemy of eternal love that superbly eliminates all fancies and sentimentalism nursled in rumour :

> The sweet, soft freshness that blooms on body's limbs—does anybody know where it was hidden so long ? Yes, when the mother was a young girl it lay pervading her heart in tender and silent mystery of love—the sweet, soft freshness that has bloomed on baby's limbs.
>
> —*Song Offerings*, LXI

Is the Poet mingled with the King of his heart whom he addresses as 'My poet' and who prepares him to listen to His 'eternal harmony' ? Born of a mystic environment his poetic delight finds a fusion in the King's words weavıng endless words in music. Here is the self-revelation of a mystic drunk in the divinely 'overflowing cup' of life :

> My poet, is it thy delight to see thy creation through my eyes and to stand at the portals of my ears silently to listen to thine own eternal harmony ?
>
> Thy world is weaving words in my mind and thy joy is adding music to them. Thou givest thyself to me in love and then feelest thine own entire sweetness in me.
>
> —*Song Offerings*, LXV

The love of the All Endearing who encloses the Poet's soul with 'colour and sounds and odours', pouring in endles cascades the joy that 'scatters and gives up and dies every moment' brings forth a mystic beyonding of gladness—an askance that haunts him unendingly. Let us be partners to the birth of this beyonding :

> Is it beyond thee to be glad with the gladness of this rhythm, to be tossed and lost and broken in the whirl of this fearful joy ?
>
> All things rush on, they stop not, they look not behind, no power can hold them back, they rush on.
>
> *Song Offerings*, LXX

The spirit of the onward march—*charaiveti*—acts as a spurt to the ardent promises, of the Poet. He is enkindled with the mystic halo of the All Beautiful and muses on :

That I should make much of myself and burn in on all sides, thus casting coloured shadows of radiance—such is thy *maya.*

Thou settest a barrier in thine own being and then callest thy sacred self in myriad notes. This thy self-preparation has taken body in me.

The poignant song is echoed through all the sky in many-coloured tears and smiles, alarms and hopes; waves rise up and sink again, dreams break and form. In me is thy own defeat of self.

—*Song Offerings*, LXXI

But the Lord's defeat of the self as the Poet believes is the beginning of the mutual high time for hide and seek. The background of this game is well set amidst the painted canvas of the night and the day. The web of mystery is wonderfully woven with the seat of the Lord rapt in mystic muse that timelessly vibrates with the muse of the Poet :

This screen that thou hast raised is painted with innumerable figures with the brush of the night and the day. Behind it thy seat is woven in wondrous mysteries of curves, casting away all barren lines of straightness.

The great pageant of thee and me has overspread the sky. With the tune of thee and me all the air is vibrant, and all ages pass with the hiding and seeking of thee and me.

—*Song Offerings*, LXXI

Is the Poet preparing himself for the farewell to this earth to meet the Lord who call him to be a partner in the journey by boat and plays on the flute the mystic muse ? With the waning of days the shadow of the evening creates an uncanny atmosphere of indecision to identify the unknown man playing upon his lute :

The day is no more, the shadow is upon the earth. It is time that I go to the stream to fill my pitcher.

The evening air is eager with the sad music of the water.

Ah, it calls me out into the dusk. In the lonely lane there is no passer-by, the wind is up, the ripples are rampant in the river.

I know not if I shall come back home. I know not whom I shall chance to meet. There at the fording of the little boat the unknown man plays upon his lute.

—*Song Offerings*, LXXIV

Already, the Poet is nearly accurate in self-assessment. He should remain standing face to face before the Lord of all worlds silently and the reason for this is well advocated in the mystic tinge of a soliloquy :

In pleasure and in pain I stand not by the side of men, and thus stand by thee. I shrink to give up my life, and thus do not plunge into the great waters of life.

—*Song Offerings*, LXXVII

To be blessed with the Lord's blessing of unison with unbroken perfection is the Poet's mystic yearning that has abundantly brought forth the 'pangs' of sorrow both in his dreams as well as in his 'wakeful hours'. His mystic prayer before the Lord is that he might bear with calm patience for the meeting with the laughter and the sound of the flute of the Lord. In the humdrum 'crowded market of this world', he therefore, takes the role of an endless waiter sitting by the roadside :

As may days pass in the crowded market of this world and my hands grow full with the daily profits, let me ever feel that I have gained nothing—let me not forget for a moment, let me carry the pangs of this sorrow in my dreams and in my wakeful hours.

When I sit by the roadside, tired and panting, when I spread my bed low in the dust, let me ever feel that the long journey is still before me—let me not forget for a moment, let me carry the pangs of this sorrow in my dreams and in my wakeful hours.

—*Song Offerings*, LXXIX

In the playhouse created by the All Beautiful the Poet has played enough and now is the time for him to bid farewell, when the mystic touch of the Master thrills him :

> In this playhouse of infinite forms I have had my play and here have I caught sight of him that is formless.
>
> My whole body and my limbs have thrilled with his touch who is beyond touch.
>
> —*Song Offerings*, XCVI

Forlorn and defeated, the Poet feels that the All Seer is seeing everything with his vision essentially mystic and beckoning him in silence to reward him with the death of welcome in the grand palace of the Eternal Master :

> From the blue sky an eye shall gaze upon me and summon me in silence. Nothing will be left for me, nothing whatever, and utter death shall I receive at thy feet.
>
> —*Song Offerings*, XCVIII

The Poet waits for the silent coming of the Lord in the dark in spite of the fact that he is defeated and forlorn, and he spreads the mat on the floor to greet the Lord face to face with mystic conversation :

> These my lamps are blown out at every little puff of wind, and trying to light them I forget all else again and again.
>
> But I shall be wise this time and wait in the dark, spreading my mat on the floor; and whenever it is thy pleasure, my Lord, come silently and take thy seat here.
>
> —*Song Offerings*, XCIX

Already, the Poet is prepared for meeting his King. The plaintive melodies from the gateway of the King have attracted him. With all brightness and lustre of the dress adorned with his 'wedding garland' he goes ahead with the great expectation of meeting his King in the mystic evening :

I shall put on my wedding garland. Mine is not the red-brown dress of the traveller, and though there are dangers on the way I have no fear in my mind.

The evening star will come out when my voyage is done and the plaintive notes of the twilight melodies be struck up from the King's gateway.

—*Song Offerings*, XCIV

A great mystic belief has already made its deep root in the heart of the Poet. He has already become familiar with the Lord and now he wants to praise the glory of his Lord with songs unending. The clash of reality and the mystic belief that he nurses in his mind very tenderly takes place in a beautiful dramatic setting. The Poet sings on the mystery of the Lord to his friends. The latter do not believe him because they have failed to spell out the secret of his song. Naturally, they scorn him and go away in utter disgust and the Poet sees his Lord sitting and smiling.

The components of the mystic muse in *Song Offerings* are, indeed, legion. Trees, birds, sea-waves, stars, the sun, the moon, the child, the flute, the boat, the light, the flowering grove, joy, pleasure, sorrow, pain and death—all are echoed with a mystic panorama of life. The matured vision of the Poet smiles in poignance and experience. He drinks the insatiable cup of joy from the infinite wonderland of Nature and shares his moments of diverse feelings with the Lord of silence.

The King of all kings sits beside him and enjoys the starry beauty of the sky only to leave him with the sense of beyond-ing, a sense for which the Poet muses in mystic vein from time immemorial. The quest for the not-yet and the thirst for knowing the unknown have enriched him a great deal to make more voyages. The beckoning of the Lord as a partner cannot be averted. The Poet himself wants the Eternal Partner to remain all along his sailing to eternity.

The play with the Lord is yet to take place in full glory. The failures on the part of the Poet are innumerable—the flute is yet to muse on the grand finale. The world is, in the mean-time, prepared to bid him farewell.

Is the Poet ready ? Is he prepared for the finest music to offer before his Lord ?

> In one salutation to thee, my God, let all my senses spread out and touch this world at thy feet.
>
> Like a rain-cloud of July hung low with its burden of unshed showers let all my mind bend down at thy door in one salutation to thee.
>
> Let all my songs gather together their diverse strains into a single current and flow to a sea of silence in one salutation to thee.
>
> Like a flock of homesick cranes flying night and day back to their mountain nests let all my life take its voyage to its eternal home in one salutation to thee.
>
> —*Song Offerings*, CIII

What a grand mystic finale !

RABINDRANATH'S QUEST FOR BEAUTY

To bathe in the beauty of creations is to be blessed with the blessings of the All Beautiful. Rabindranath Tagore, an incomparable worshipper of beauty throughout his life, sought beauty not extrinsically but essentially introspectively and the sense of beauty appears in his creations as a living, dynamic force. As the fountain of beauty is the heart, his quest for beauty is primarily in the heart's paradise. He seeks the reasons for the blooming beauty of creation within himself and finds the indomitable force within as quite inexplicable. However, he makes an explanation in his own inimitable fashion on the inner urge for beauty that makes a new history of human creative process :

> I do not know who goes on painting the portrait of life on the canvas of reminiscence. But whoever paints it, he paints portraits alone. This means : whatever is happening does not necessarily require to be painted with a brush to have a true copy. Oh, what he eliminates or retains in accordance with his own likings ! How he belittles the great or enlarges the little ones ! He does not slightly hesitate to arrange the rear in place of the front or *vice versa*. In fact, his only assignment is to paint portraits and not to write history.
>
> —Rabindranath Tagore : *Jeevansmriti* (*Reminiscence of Life*), Visva-Bharati, 1971, p. 1.
>
> [Translated by me]

Like a faithful creative artist of beauty, Tagore believes in unfolding the inherent mystery of beauty as and when it appears before him in spontaneity. Perhaps he greatly believes in the truth of Bacon's statement that the best part of beauty is that which no picture can express. Therefore, the quest becomes a haunting one—a thrilling and unending voyage in the sea of beauty.

Right from the beginning of the manifestation of his creative excellence, Rabindranath shows his extraordinary power of unveiling the beauty of the evening in a superb poetic splendour of imageries. The evening personified and endeared by the Poet quite lovingly is in happy unison with a poetic mind yearning for a duet :

O Evening,
Under the endless sky sitting alone
with dishavelled hair
What mild conversation do you make in your own mind
In singing
By looking at the sky
Everyday have I heard even today your words
I've failed to follow.
Everyday have I heard even today your song
I've failed to learn.
My eyes are swooned in drowsiness
My heart awaits dawn
From the farthest horizon of the heart
Harmonizing your voice with mine
The vacant alien one
Sings as if your own song with you.

—Rabindranath Tagore : "Sandhya" ("The Evening"), *Sandhyasangeet*, *Rabindra-Rachanavali*, Volume I, Government of West Bengal, Calcutta, 1980, p. 5.
[Translated by me]

The romantic discovery of the beauty of love as the Poet makes at a very young age in his poetic creation *Sandhya-sangeet* takes the reader to a serene land of artistic beauty. One cannot but, for example, recall the dramatic moment of beauty as manifested in the portrait of love drawn in the canvas of the morning with the nostalgic aroma of the union between the lover and the beloved with the eternal askance of love :

Once if the girl came not
Inactive would, as if, the heart be
The morning would not pass
The day would trek on in feet desolate
The cycle of years came again
The earth again laughed in spring
In the morning seated under the trees
Said I to Damini in course of conversation
'Damini, my darling, do you love me ?'

—Rabindranath Tagore : "Vish O Sudha" ("Poison and Hemlock"), *Sandhyasangeet*, *Rabindra-Rachanavali*, Vol. I, Government of West Bengal, Calcutta 1980, p. 50.

[Translated by me]

Side by side with this romantic quest for love, the Poet makes a realistic appeal that unnerves the memory with the melancholy mood of the sorrow that tears apart the romance in the rude shock of death of the dearest sister, Malati. The soliloquy here rings in the innermost core of the heart and reveals the truth that shatters the quest for mere romance in love :

O poisonous, fiery, thunderous love,
Cover your face before this affection !
The insect of death you are, the Satan of life,
Like a fire you are in the beauteous forest of flowers,
Disease of the heart, you nursle
Thirst in the heart all the time,
Encompassing the snakelike clasping of your hand
You go on breathing out poisonous air,
Fired with your volcanic breath
The heated current of blood blooms on !

* * * * *

This love, this poison, this thundering fire—
When would this bid farewell to this earth ?
Come ye affection, come showering your pleasant stream of juice,

Put out this burning heap of fire !
From the firy clasp of the scorpion
Take up in your lap drenched with juice.
Younder in the sky the comet of love is up
Flashing the eye, alas, of youth.
Where are you, the Pole star, rise for once
Pour in this burning eye your lustre pleasant and soft
Hemlock you are, a shadow, the stream of moonlight,
A rivulet, the air of the dawn,
Laughter you are, hope and tears mild,
Come and put out this love.
One who has one Malati in his family
A thousand Damini is not equal to her bowl of dust !

—*Ibid.*, pp. 55-66.
[Translated by me]

The quest for the beauty of death in creative force appears in a new pattern of poetic consciousness in *Prabhatsangeet*. In fact, in the preface to this book of poems, the Poet plunges into self-revelation in a very easy fashion :

Looking within my heart, an idea awoke within me that everything good and evil of my every moment, my all experiences of joy and sorrow of day to day life are taking an endless image of creation ceaselessly. The real nature of that creativity is the eternal ups and downs of this expression and non-expression. Thinking over this, it seemed to me : What, then, is the meaning of death ? Somehow the reply was that life retains everything while death leads. I am dying at every moment and through this death I am marching ahead towards the avenue of life. It is as if the work of sowing is going on within me—the past, present, and future are being sewn.

—Rabindranath Tagore : "Prabhatsangeet" : Preface, *Rabindra-Rachnavali*, Vol. I, Government of West Bengal, Calcutta, 1980, p. 61.

[Translated by me]

The quest for eternal beauty in the echo representing time and life and death as expressed in "Pratidhwani" ("The

Echo") is a wonderful pattern of imagery with which the Poet presents his readers :

O Echo,
I understand I love you
I understand I love none else
You have made me eager and restless
My *Veena* weeps for you
Hearing the songs of birds in your mouth,
The murmuring of the fountain
The song of the intense mysterious forest
The pleasant voice of the lad
Hearing from you the music of the world
I have loved you
Yet, why do I not see you ?
I have searched you throughout the world.

* * * * *

Until death, unendingly shall I seek you,
Shall I not have your trace ?
Will you only remain away, from a very great distance,
Shall I not hear that faint music ?
Standing amid this world
The flute of beauty will you play on
In the endless track of life shall I go on
Seeking you,
Vacant will be the heart and the mind.

—Rabindranath Tagore : "Pratidhwani" ("The Echo"), *Prabhat Sangeet*, *Rabindra-Rachanavali*, Vol. I, Government of West Bengal, Calcutta, 1980, p. 80-83.

[Translated by me]

The echo of life that the Poet feels in his heart finds further outlet in the exposure of beauty in the description of the morning as he depicts in "Prabhat-Utsav" ("The Ceremony of the Morning") :

The honey of the pleasant is the light, the honey of the pleasant is the wind.
The rivulet runs with the honey-sweet song
Wherever the eye looks, it goes on seeing alone

Whoever it sees it calls him nearer
The eye sinks on the edges of dewlike eyes
The heart sinks in the sea of joy.

—Rabindranath Tagore : "Prabhat-Utsav" (The Ceremony of the Morning"), *Prabhat Sangeet, Rabindra-Rachanavali*, Vol. I, Government of West Bengal, Calcutta, p. 71.

[Translated by me]

The quest for the beauty of love that adorns every object of Nature goes on quite convincingly and the Poet makes an unforgettable experience in seeing and enjoying the stars and the night. The words he uses for his description open out a new horizon of beauty. This is further emphasizing the fact that the Poet has an inward eye of beauty that has its parallel only in that of Victor Hugo who is re-enlivened in Tagore's translation.

The words of dedication as the Poet uses for his book of Poems "Chhabi O Gaan" ("Pictures and Songs") are worthy embodiments of the quest for beauty. In fact, the spring of beauty re-appears in a new garb in these poems, and the Poet plunges into the beautiful and mysterious world of Nature quite cordially and psychologically to reveal the beauty of the Great Creator of the world. In this quest for beauty, Tagore makes new experimentations in language and diction. As he concludes his Preface to the book :

Let me say what I would like to say about "Chhabi O Gaan". It is written at the time of adolescence when childhood and youth have just synchronized. There is childishness in language and in ideas, youth. Before that, a sense of pain was inherent. It has as if, wanted to pacify itself in delirium. Now that age * * has gone out to find the form.

—Rabindranath Tagore : "Chhabi O Gaan" ("Pictures and Songs"); Preface, *Rabindra-Rachanavali* Government of West Bengal, Calcutta, 1980, Vol. I, p. 117.

[Translated by me]

Joyous and youthful as the Poet is, the form of poetry appears in beauty with many-sided splendour in his creation.

The creative spontaneity at this stage of his life gets a new spurt in solemn askance and enquiry into the spirit of beauty. The lovely scene of the lover and the beloved with the approach of the evening is drawn with a mystic touch of union in beyonding this earth :

Darkness came in
The birds slept
The golden sunlight was in unison with the sky
The clouds departed towards eternity
And the twain swing a-sitting,
Come closer to breast each other
In fusion with each other's mouth
Encompassing with arms
Slowly is the breath falling
Now and then with intervals,
Looking at the sky, they see
The two stars at the backdrop of the tree
Where does the heart fly, O where
It rushes towards those stars
It gets lost in the sky
  Leaving the earth
  They have as if become two stars.

—Rabindranath Tagore : "Dola" ("The Swing"), *Chhabi O Gaan*, *Rabindra-Rachanavali*, Vol. I, Government of West Bengal, Calcutta 1980, p. 123.

[Translated by me]

Elsewhere, the beauty of the lover and the beloved set in the backdrop of a drowsy landscape and the beloved's weaving of a song to greet the lover in smile while fast asleep in intoxication make an unparalleled scene of love in beauty :

Let's go to the river-bank
Sitting there slowly
Do you play on a flute only
The moon will smile in the sky
In your sweet voice slowly
Do you sing a song of happiness only.

* * * * *

O maiden, by singing
Do you keep woven the garland of *Malati*
While asleep, garland him.
The fragrance of the flowers will unite in dream
Keep staring at the sleeping face with love
The mild smile will flower in the face.

—Rabindranath Tagore : "Matal" ("The Intoxicated"), *Chhabi O Gaan*, *Rabindra-Rachanavali*, Vol. I, Government of West Bengal, Calcutta, 1980, p. 135.

[Translated by me]

The Poet makes continuous experiments with his renewed concept of beauty and the quest goes on. One of the experiments refers to his genius in exploring the element of love in his *Bhanusingha Thakurer Padavali* that has undergone long years of poetic endeavour. In fact, there is a soft corner for this creative manifestation in his heart and the romantic aura of his imagination is spread on the canvas of a mellow atmosphere of love. One of the finest imageries of love is revealed in the exotic muse beginning with "Amid the dense flower grove" :

Amid the dense flower grove
Mild and pleasant does the flute play on
Forgetting fear and public shame
  Come, O dear, come.
With costume decent and blue on the body
With heaps of flowers of love in the heart
With eyes like a deer and laughter serene
  Come, O come, in the flower grove.

—Rabindranath Tagore : "Amid the dense flower grove" (No. 8), *Bhanusingha Thakurer Padavali*, *Rabindra-Rachanavali*, Vol. I, Government of West Bengal, Calcutta, 1980, p. 172.

[Translated by me]

The poet's quest for beauty as reflected in *Bhanusingher Padavali* associated with a very sordid and delicate poignance of pain. The very words of dedication to his beloved who is no more reveal the truth :

> Many a time you requested me to publish the poems of Bhanusingha. Then I did not comply with that request. I have published it today, and today you could not see any more.
>
> —*Ibid.*, p. 163
> [Translated by me]

In *Kadi O Komal* where the Poet discovers beauty in a newer pattern, the youthful vigour in him finds a new language of exposition. In his own comment titled "Kabir Mantabya" ("The comment of the Poet") at the beginning of the book of poems as a preface, he explains his own position quite frankly :

> Youth is that time of the change of season in the life when the unexposed enthusiasm for blooming and perfection suddenly becomes visible in manifold colours and appearances. *Kadi O Komal* is my composition of that youth anew. * * * * Whatever found expression within me was new and sincere to me also.
>
> —Rabindranath Tagore: *Kadi O Kamal*, "Kabir Mantabya" ("The comment of the Poet"), *Rabindra-Rachanavali*, Government of West Bengal, Calcutta, 1980, Vol. I, p. 191.
> [Translated by me]

Despite vibrant and youthful, the poignance of beauty in mystic aura of love in some of the poems here makes a new departure in romanticism and the Poet presents a serene picture of love in an exquisite language. "Bhavisyater Rangabhumi" ("The Playground of the Future") proves the point. Let us have the following mystic perfume :

> Who are making us play in our playhouse
> Ere the play is over, we came back in the eve,
> Where have you thrown that room of dust away ?
> Here, where we two sat
> The heavenly union in laughter and tears was made,
> What a sea of words we wrote by tracing on the sand,
> Who you are that wiped those endearing writings !
> That sweet girl would roll on the ground here,
> When kissed, her smile would spread a-bloom

For that the *madhavi* creeper raised her head here
Thought I she would for ever remain a-bloom
O where and who has trampled her !

—Rabindranath Tagore : *Kadi O Komal*, "Bhavisyater Rangabhumi" ("The Playground of the Future"), *Rabindra-Rachanavali*, Government of West Bengal, Calcutta, 1980, Vol. I, p. 202.

[Translated by me]

From the poignance of beauty delineated as above, the Poet takes us back to a rather mellow atmosphere of love born in the womb of time and nursled in the language of reminiscence :

Where is the shadow of the tree, the green affection of the forest !
Embracing the trees on the banks with ripples all day long.
Away towards the lovely home does the stream advance
Where is the shadow of the tree, the green affection of the forest !
Where in the deep blue the end of the forest is in unison
The eyes lose vision in the endless sphere of eternity
The wind comes from the distance and away goes to the distant land
The muse goes a-floating, where do they go !
The laughter, the flute and the jokes, the pure happy breaths
The union all the year on the green banks of the stream
Some play or swing or sleep on the lap of the shadow
The day runs on towards the rippling stream
Some pluck *Vakul*, some prepare the garland.
Like a shade in the shadow some go on singing
Someone is silently whispering somewhere
The hair is dishavelled, she has forgotten to knot
She has held aloft in fingers lest the eyes are covered
The bangle is unloosened, she is keeping in the shadow of the tree

Amid the forest murmur the lonely flute plays on
With that tuning sing the two doves at times.

—*Ibid.* "*Vaner Chhaya*" ("The Shadow of the Forest"), p. 203.

[Translated by me]

Unlimited as the Poet's yearning is, he seeks the last word for the fullest exposition of himself. Is it the fruit of his quest for beauty ? In "*Sesh Katha*" ("The Last Word"), the concluding poem of *Kadi O Komal*, the Poet spells out his hypothesis :

I think some last word is there
The word that makes all clear
* * * * *
The word that will myself reveal
In my own words shall I greatly feel.

—*Ibid.* "*Sesh Katha*" ("The Last Word"), p. 279.

[Translated by me]

The search for the word of the heart that the Poet makes, leads him towards greater and more thrilling quest for beauty. He makes himself continually prepared for the most unassuming but the most appropriate word for self-revelation and self-discovery. Rich and varied as his experience was in the wonderland of creative sensibilities, he could easily switch over from one pattern of imagery to the other. These variations are found in plenty in his *Manasi* where every poem is a romantic endeavour into the quest for beauty. The first poem of this book, for example, is a frank revelation of this truth :

Amid this silent mind often sounds
  The wavy stroke of the world
Therefore, in the sounding heart no rest is there
  Sleepless is the day and night
The voice of the song of joy and sorrow is continually heard
  The sound alone, and no language is there
The manifold murmurs make me restless,
  Manifold vain hopes do me awake
And so all thro' this life I have nothing to do
  Save composing the limit of the endless

With hope and language, pouring love with them,
I build up the image of my mind.

—Rabindranath Tagore : "*Upahar*" ("The Gift"), *Manasi*, *Rabindra-Rachanavali*, Government of West Bengal, Calcutta, 1980, Vol. I, p. 303.

[Translated by me]

How does the image of his mind respond? Let us be, for the time being, partners to the Poet's quest for the beauty in her :

I could portray you hold you within me
Beneath the shade of the pangs of pain in lovely cool
Sometimes I see your faded face
Sometimes laughter wells up in the banks of your eyes
Sometimes holding your palms throughout the night
I remain encompassed in your dress and hair.

—Rabindranath Tagore: "*Virahananda*", *Manasi*, *Rabindra-Rachanavali*, Government of West Bengal, Calcutta, 1980, Vol. I, p. 309.

[Translated by me]

Nature personified in the Poet's quest for beauty finds a new expression in the exposition of love that transcends from romanticism to mysticism. The deep sense of the quest for beauty in love as set forth in the appropriate ornaments of language in "Prakritir Prati" ("Towards Nature") turns everything dramatic in soliloquy :

I understand not whom you love
Or neglect
Whom you lovingly entertain
In the morn
Unto the dust
Unremembered
Does he become in the evening.

—*Ibid.* "Prakritir Prati" ("Towards Nature"), p. 324.

[Translated by me]

The Poet also runs wild towards Nature, despite the fact that he is running towards her in futility. He also makes a deep study of the smile in her face that spreads the mysterious aura of her intentions of love-offerings and interprets her beauty of the star-studded sky :

Spreading my mind and the heart, I rush towards you
But you appear not
The sunny smile mild in approach
Is seen in your sunlike lips
If far away do I want to depart
You keep awake with your trap
What a strategy what a force
The restless and vibrant you are !
Know you not your bounds
And mysteries
And so, at blind night when the seven worlds
Remain asleep,
Stealthily and curiously
Do you stand under the sky
Trimming hundreds and millions of
Starry light.

—*Ibid.*, pp. 324-325
[Translated by me]

The Poet seeks the mystery of beauty even in the voice of the cuckoo and in his own imagery of the goddess of Beauty :

Some is as if seated nearby the chest of the world
The simple, beautiful maiden
As if that embodiment of beauty, the *Saraswati* of music
Is holding the hypnotizing *Veena.*

—Rabindranath Tagore : "*Kuhudhwani*", *Manasi*, *Rabindra-Rachanavali*, Government of West Bengal, Calcutta, 1281, Vol. I, p. 329.

[Translated by me]

The beauty of Bengal as exposed through the poems of *Sonar Tari* (*The Golden Boat*) is the Poet's own concept of beauty buoyant in the resonance of his romantic period of creativity. He himself gives the reasons for his likings for the beauty of Bengal in a very artistic way :

To ask a poet to explain the specialities in excitement of poetry of a particular nature in a particular period of life is to harass him. How will he know ? The inherent mystery of the changes that take place in the growth of life is not easily revealed. All the branches of trees do not spread towards the same direction, they move by turning and twisting themselves. Its scientific reason is hidden in the sky, air, light and on earth. If the tree would have thought over it, yet it would not have found berth in the assembly of the ministry of the process of creation. It would not have the right to cast its vote. It only takes everything to be accepted. This is its duty by nature. The biologist who is seated outside can rather provide many informations.* * There is novelty in infinity. Its very beckoning came to me. The mind responded to it, whatever was already hidden in branches like buds began to bloom in light. But the writings of *Sonar Tari* (*The Golden Boat*) are made with a different background. I was roaming in the rivers and the villages of Bengal at that time. Its novelty is that of dynamic diversity.* * At times, much more of the language and the tune entered the inmost core of my mind in diverse appearances than whatever came visible to me. I was having that reception of continual acquaintance in my heart.

—Rabindranath Tagore : *Sonar Tari* (*The Golden Boat*) Introduction, *Rabindra Rachanavali*, Government of West Bengal, Calcutta, 1980, Vol I, p. 435.

[Translated by me.]

The delight of the mystery of Nature that the Poet enjoys in abundance finds its superb manifestation in the poems of *Sonar Tari.* The exposure of beauty made in the poem "*Vimvavati*" through a contrastic setting and dramatic strategy is a fine explantation of the Poet's exploration of beauty. The last stanza of this poem is a thrilling climax that serenely welcomes the unavoidable truth of beauty :

The golden headgear the Queen began to rub
With sand. The reflection still remained.
She besmeared with ink but unaffected the picture was

She trimmed fire in it but the gold melt not
She threw it on the ground with tremendous force
But the mystic mirror broke not. On the ground
The Queen fell all on a sudden and life came to an end
The diamonds and the jewels like fire
Began to burn. Beside her on the ground
Two laughing faces smile in her golden mirror
Vimvavati, the step daughter of the Queen.
The most beautiful of all on earth.

—Rabindranath Tagore : "*Vimvavati*", *Sonar Tari* (*The Golden Boat*), *Rabindra-Rachanavali*, Government of West Bengal, Calcutta, 1980, Vol. I, p. 440.

[Translated by me]

On a different context, of course, the same sense of beauty is revealed in the poem "Paras-Pathar' ("The Touchstone"). Here the Poet enters rather more deeply into the concept of beauty and the vehicle for the manifestation of beauty, is a simple, self-disinterested '*khaypa*' ('The homeless') who is in continual search of the real, the touchstone. The marks of simplicity are all evident in his appearance and manners. The beautiful portrait of Nature is drawn with a vivid aroma of serenity in the backdrop of a great philosophy of life in renunciation of the ephemeral objects of nature :

The faded sun was then setting out
The golden sky with the gold of the melted sea,
The bride of the western horizon sees golden dreams
The saint slowly goes back again towards the east
To seek the lost gem anew.
No more strength he has, the burden of the body slumps down
Like a torn tree does the heart drop down
The old long way like a dead man does lie
Now end it has, away it goes.
From horizon to horizon the sands of the desert seem alone

Ematiated is everyland with the shadow of the imminent
night

—Rabindranath Tagore : "*Paras-Pathar*" ("The Touchstone"), *Rabindra-Rachanavali*, Government of West Bengal, Calcutta, 1980, Vol. I, p, 460.

[Translated by me]

The beauty of the silent night set against the background of a mysterious atmosphere adds a new dimension to the Poet's quest for beauty. The poverty of affluence find a new language in renunciation, the '*Khaypa*' shows the way adroitly but the poignance of atmosphere accompanies quite unassumingly. As a matter of fact, Tagore in the endeavour for the quest for beauty breaks a new ground in *Sonar Tari* with judicious unison of imageries and artistic sensibilities. Poetry, the beautiful beloved of his mind as the Poet imagines, takes a new turn in romantic personification. The address of welcome is rather sensual but the sense of thrilling desire pulsates in expression :

O Beautiful of my mind, come leaving the *Veena*
Only with a clasp of your empty hands
Adorn my neck—with a touch of your lotus-like hands
Romance springs up with inmost exhilaration
The trembling and restless breast, the watery eyes,
The enamoured limbs crumble down, the heart alone
On the edge of the limb flashes out
As if the tie of sensuality will tear apart.

—Rabindranath Tagore : "*Manas Sundari*", *Sonar Tari*, *Rabindra-Rachanavali*, Government of West Bengal, Calcutta, 1980, Vol. I, p. 480.

[Translated by me]

The complication of love is well portrayed in the alchemy of sensual beauty :

Smiling slowly,
Looking at me. O mysteriously sweet !
What do you want to tell me, O intoxicated in love
My Endless, what do you want to make me realize ?
No words are needed, only wrap up

My whole body and mind with your covering
Steal me completely with your force.
My all, with breast upon your naked breast
Let me, O dear, listen to the mystery of the heart

—*Ibid.*, p. 484.
[Translated by me]

The echo of John Donne's quest for beauty is heard : What covering do you require more than a man ?

But Tagore goes a step further in his quest for beauty with volleys of askance that breathes a sombre air of the thirsty heart :

Know, know I, my beloved friend,
If we both meet face to face
In the avenue of after-life, startlingly would we stand
The sleeping past will tremble up like a lightning
With consciousness. Know I that methinks
Like a polestar throughout the life
These black eyes ever familiar
Taking light from my eyes,
Intentions from my heart,
My secret love is composed
With that face. Would you also
Recognize me intrinsically ? Would we two
Unite ?

—*Ibid.*, p. 487.
[Translated by me]

And, when the romantic reverie of beauty is over, the Poet welcomes in a dramatic denouement :

Come Sleep, Come Peace,
Come, O dear, with beauty enamoured, silent, plaintive,
Pull me in your breast, with care
Place me on the bed lovely in death, white and enriched
in oblivion.

—*Ibid.*, p. 488.
[Translated by me]

The agonies of love in isolation as the Poet expresses in

the poem "*Vyrtha Jouvan*" ("The Baffled Youth") find a new avenue of excellence in beauty. The whole Nature speaks up in support of the love lost in the lonely night in the absence of the beloved :

It seemed as if she has called me
As if she has remembered me for ever
With devotion to the brim, she will come
And make the river of youth aware,
She will come at night and tie me with the knot of love
Ah, that night passes on, how shall I call it back ?

—Rabindranath Tagore : "*Vyrtha Jouvan*" (The Baffled Youth"), *Sonar Tari*, *Rabindra-Rachanavali*, Government of West Bengal, Calcutta, 1980, Vol. I, p. 505.
[Translated by me]

The etertnal askance of beauty that haunts the Poet's mind finds manifestation in all excellence in "Journey to the Unknown"—"*Niruddesh Jatra*". Symbolic as the imagery appears, the romantic vein touches the inmost core of the heart with a 'longing lingering look' to rediscover the Beautiful :

How far away would you take me along,
O Beautiful ?
Tell me on which bank your
golden boat would embark
When asked, O alien
Smile you alone, O sweet smiling one,
I understand not what you feel
within your mind.
Silently you show me by raising your finger.
The shoreless sea is surging
Yonder is the western sun setting in the
corner of the sky
What is here ? In whose quest am I marching onward ?

—Rabindranath Tagore : "*Niruddesh Yatra*", (The Journey to the Unknown"), *Rabindra-Rachanavali*, Government of West Bengal, Calcutta, 1981, Vol. I, p. 541.
[Translated by me]

The quest for beauty as the Poet makes in *Sonar Tari* (*The Golden Boat*) undergoes a radical change in *Chitra* where beauty adds to divine grace. Tagore himself gives a very lucid explanation in introduction to this book of poems :

> I felt a dual existence of myself. It is something like the joint existence of stars, that is within my own personality. Its very attraction is strong. Its very resolution is being fulfilled through me, through my joy and sorrow, good and evil, the one 'I' in this pursuit of resolution is an instrument and the other 'I' may be an agent of instrument but the music that comes out is the original characteristic of the instrument that forms a fundamental part. At every step, the compromise goes on and the two in union makes creation. It is as if a feeling of half woman and half God.
>
> —Rabindranath Tagore : "*Chitra*", Introduction, *Rabindra-Rachanavali*, Government of West Bengal, Calcutta, 198), Vol. I, p. 559.
>
> [Translated by me]

The title poem "*Chitra*", a mouthpiece of the Poet's concept of beauty, begins with the manifold exposures of beauty :

How diverse you are in this world
O the embodiment of diversities !
With unending light are you shining in the blue sky
With rapturous delight are you laughing in the flower-garden
In heaven and on earth are you treading with moving feet
O you, the restless traveller.

—*Ibid.*, "*Chitra*", p. 561.
[Translated by me]

The beauty of love as a beauty in divine grace gets a new expression in "*Premer Abhishek*" where love is in unison with romantic sexuality but crystallized in purity :

I have treasured with care your touch and your love
Your message from the pleasant voice, your kiss,
The vision of your eyes with all the body and the mind filled in

* * * *

O magnanimous, you have made me an emperor.

—Rabindranath Tagore : "*Premer Abhishek*" ("The Commemoration of Love"), *Chitra, Rabindra-Rachanavali*, Government of West Bengal, Calcutta, 1980, Vol. I, p. 567.

[Translated by me]

The thirsty heart of the Poet in search of the beauty of love becomes rather benign in tone and approach. The longings are limited as it is aptly revealed in "*Piyashi*" ("The Thirsty") :

But I want nothing
I only remained standing
Behind the forest bending down my head
Even then the idle sun of dawn
Was with enmeshed eyes
Even then the air was drenched
With the dew-drops of night
The fragrance of new grass
Does the morning breeze bear
Alone, out of the cottage,
Under the shade of *Asath*
Are you seated

* * *

But I did not go nearby
Know not I what the restless wind
Has made your hair
The bell was then ringing in the courtyard
The sky was waking up
Towards the sky the earth was looking up
Praying for God's blessings

* * *

Your bangles continually ring
The milk foams up

With a thirsty eyes, did I remain in a corner,
The heart aggrieved in silence.

—Rabindranath Tagore : "*Piyashi*" ("The Thirsty") *Kalpana*, *Rabindra-Rachanavali*, Government of West Bengal, Calcutta, 1980, Vol. I, pp. 805-806.

[Translated by me]

The beauty of the pangs of separation as expressed in "*Viraha*" is a natural come back on the part of the Poet in the world of pure romanticism. The language is lucid and vibrant, the imagery woven in the thread of simplicity :

When you went away
It was noon then.
The sun was in the mid-sky
The sunlight brighter.
Finishing home work
In the lonely room I then remained
Seated alone on the window
At that time you departed
Then it was noon.

* * * *

When you departed
It was noon then.
The dried path, the burnt field,
The sunlight brighter
In the dense shade of the branch of a bunyan tree
The two doves call on and on
In the window I was alone
Vacant is the bed-room
When you went away
It was noon, then.

—Rabindranath Tagore : "*Viraha*", *Kshanika*, *Rabindra-Rachanavali*, Government of West Bengal, Calcutta, 1980, Vol. I, pp. 917-918.

[Translated by me]

The sense of beauty finds in the absence of the beloved a new vision of love in waiting for the day of union.

If 'our sweetest songs are those that tell of saddest thought' as Shelley concludes in "The Skylark", Tagore makes the same conclusion of sweetness and beauty in his exposition of love in bereavement. Here is the mournful yearning for love with all inherent beauty :

> Like a guest the mad days of the spring come so many times
> With *Veena* in her hands she came smiling in front of doors yours and mine
>
> * * * *
>
> No more you are today, she came with the southern wind
> I fail to remain forgetful about her for a moment today
> She is bringing your vision, your message unexpressed
> She is murmuring your aching mind in the garden
> I was a truant on the day of union with her
> And now your separation brings her through repeated calls in the vacant room
>
> —Rabindranath Tagore : *Smaran* ('*Remembrance*') *Rabindra-Rachanavali*, Government of West Bengal, Calcutta, 1980, Vol. I, Poem No. 19, p. 1022.
>
> [Translated by me]

The bereaved heart of the Poet seeks beauty in void and this sense of beauty is created not in isolation with Nature but essentially endearing Nature as an embodiment of nostalgia—a reminiscence eternal. The woes of the lover and the beloved, even in isolation, are alive in all natural perspectives and even the vacant room throbs again with beautiful movements and conversations that haunt the Poet's mind time and again.

Beauty with her mellow touch appears in abundance in Tagore's *Sishu* (*The Child*). Undoubtedly a new dimension in the quest for beauty, here the Poet himself is a child playing on in innocence with the beautiful objects of Nature. But along with the eternal play of the child on the sea-shore of eternity, beauty appears in deeper concepts also. Hide and seek is the emblem of this quest eternal. The Poet unfolds the mystery of beauty in the autobiographical vein of a child spreading the oysters of beauty before the sea-shore of humanity. Here is a description of a child in action in the evening marked with all serenity of beauty :

At dusk by trimming the light
To the cowshed when you will come
Then I, playing the game of flowers
Will suddenly wither on the ground.
Again shall I be your child
'Tell me stories' I shall tell you.
'Where had you been, naughty boy ?' You would say.
'I won't tell you' will be my reply.

—Rabindranath Tagore : "*Lookochuri*" ("Hide and Seek"), *Sishu* (*The Child*), *Rabindra-Rachanavali*, Government of West Bengal, Calcutta, 1980, Vol. II, p. 39.

[Translated by me]

The mysterious reply of the child : 'I won't tell you' rings endlessly and the mind seeks the answer in all his beauteous activities and movements that appear like the eternal muse of the All Beautiful. The Poet goes deeper and deeper within the core of his heart, but, apparently, he shows signs of simplicity and boisterous nature like a child to become his continual, playful partner. The sense of sombre attitude is engulfed with a deep veil of joyous activities that never allow a child to remain aloof from the kingdom of Beauty.

The elements of beauty arising out of the brisk activities of the child do not get lost in the melee of human activities. The Poet has a keen eye and a kind heart, too. He cannot be rude to the child despite his naughtiness nor can he become indifferent to his views and opinions. He allows himself to suffer from conflicts consequential to affection and awareness, duty and forbearance as internal components of beauty. Indeed, it is a quest of all quests for beauty. Let us take part in the judicious arguments of the child who is in fact, the spokesman of the Poet himself suffering from conflicts of duty :

When father writes
You tell not anything

Doesn't he spoil
Heaps of paper everyday ?
If I want to build my paper-boat
Immediately you react : 'Don't spoil.'
Is it better
To tarnish white papers with black hues ?

—Rabindranath Tagore : "*Samalochak*" ("The Critic"), *Sishu* (*The Child*), *Rabindra-Rachanavali*, Government of West Bengal, Calcutta, 1980, Vol. II, p. 25.
[Translated by me]

Perhaps the irony of beauty trampled by the so-called sane humanity has its exposure in the frank statement of the child who has a clear vision of the massacres of human destruction, pleading for the joy and beauty of creativity. Moreover, the silent listener, the mother, is juxtaposed to allow avenues for emancipation of creative efflorescence in the face of untoward circumstances. The agonies of bullying childhood in the peril of beauty and creativity did not avert the Poet's attention.

The quest for beauty is the quest for the Poet's own philosophy of life. As Tagore gives a self-explanation :

The fragrance that trembles before
the breast of the flower
The song that remains in slumber in the light of dawn
The lustre that dances in beckonings with the autumnal paddy
And laughs with the gold and green in light
That fragrance has my frame built
That song has woven in me this new *maya*
The lustre has cast shadow upon my eyes
Who can hold me within.

—Rabindranath Tagore : *Utsarga* (*Dedication*), *Rabindra-Rachanavali*, Government of West Bengal, Calcutta, 1980, Vol. II, Poem No. 21, p. 81
[Translated by me]

An apostle of beauty himself, Tagore makes an ardent and sincere revelation of beauty in fusion with finer elements of

Nature—the fragrance of flowers, the song sealed in slumber and the variegated lustre of light. Like beauty changeable from time to time, the Poet remains out of the ordinary bounds of humanity and his creative beauty casts its infinite spell upon all objects of Nature and mankind as well. The mystery is further deepened with creative beauty spread over the endless joy and sorrow, pleasure and pain, good and evil of this ever changing world.

The quest for beauty is further accentuated in *Gitanjali* where Beauty is personified and given a mystic interpretation.

Beauty, you came in the morning today,
With sun-hued *Parijat* in your hands
The sleeping castle, no passer-by on the way
In the golden chariot you left alone
Stopping for a while towards the window
You glanced with your eyelids plaintive
Beauty, you came in the morning, today.

In what fragrance was my dream filled
In what joy the darkness of the room trembled
Silent is my *veena* that trampled in the dust
And with what an unwounded stroke did it play on

Many a time was I about to rise
Leaving indolence run out towards the way.
When I awoke, you departed
No more, I think, would we meet again
Beauty, you came in the morning, today.

—Rabindranath Tagore : *Gitanjali*, *Rabindra-Rachanavali*, Government of West Bengal, Calcutta, 1980, Vol. II, Poem No. 67, p. 234.

[Translated by me]

Although there is an uncanny feeling of beauty in the mind of the Poet, he firmly believes that the offerings he makes for the manifestation of beauty of All Beautiful will endear the inmost heaven of perfection with every avenue of excellence. The muse goes on with the aroma of beyonding of beauty—a quest perennial.

The idea of this perennial quest finds a new exposition in the very opening lines of "*Geetimalya*" (The *Garland of Songs*) where the Poet plays, with beauteous artistry, the role of a mystic meditating on the beyonding of consciousness :

Where the night mingles
With the sea of day
On that juncture we two
Did unite
The black and the white
Are in unison there
With darkness and light
There the waves are running
Between the shores
Amid the depthless blue silence
The sombre message played on
Unalloyed did bloom
The line of gold
I prepare to look at the face
I am about to see but I cannot see
I awake enraptured with dream
I cry with endless tears.

—Rabindranath Tagore : *Geetimalya* (*The Garland of Songs*) *Rabindra-Rachanavali*, Government of West Bengal, Calcutta, 1980, Vol. II, No. 1, p. 295.

[Tanslated by me]

The tears of the Poet appear pearl-like in humility and poignance of mystic beauty. The not-yet—*adhara*—mingles in all beauty and the quest is represented in the symbolic expression of running from one sea-shore of humanity to the other, What a grace in persistent endeavour !

The quest for beauty, as the Poet believes, is waiting for eternity and the waiting for eternity is the joy unending. Like Wordsworth who believes in seeing 'into the life of things', Tagore also loves in seeing and enjoying the world with all its varied beauty. As he sings,

My joy lies in seeing
along this path
The sunshine and the shadow
play on

The rains and the Spring
Arrive
Who come and go
In front of me
Bringing the message
Pleased am I within me
Gently blows the wind
With eyes wide open
Shall I remain alone in the door
When all on a sudden
the auspicious moment will come.
The meeting will take place.
Meanwhile, at times
Sing I and smile aside
By then at intervals
The beautiful fragrance floats along
Seeing along the path does my joy lie.

—Rabindranath Tagore : *Geetimalya* (*The Garland of Songs*), *Rabindra-Rachanavali*, Government of West Bengal, Calcutta, 1980, Vol. II, No. 7, p. 300.

[Translated by me]

Does the Poet believe in the quest for beauty as the journey eternal ? Let us listen to his own confession :

My journey is for many years
And towards a great distance
Out I came first
In the first chariot of light
With planets and stars in curved lines
I painted my foot-prints
On so many forests and mountains
of human habitations and beyond

—Rabindranath Tagore : *Geetimalya* (*The Garland of Songs*). *Rabindra-Rachanavali*, Government of West Bengal, Calcutta, 1980, Vol. III, No. 14, p. 307.

[Translated by me]

As the quest remains incomplete, the ardent desire of the Poet to encounter Beauty endearingly bewails in the eternal askance 'Where, O Where ?'

'Ah, here you are !' To say
These words
I feasted my eyes in so many direction
In so many ways
To fill in the world in millions of streams
Flows on the current of 'you are, you are'
'Where you are, O where' ! melts in recent tears.

—*Ibid.*, p. 308

[Translated by me]

The inner wailing of the Poet's heart seeks beauty in the love of the All Beautiful. The world appears to him as the embodiment of the All Beautiful. He welcomes the world with his love that came like a song and was in happy unison for eternity. Quite convincingly, the Poet observes :

O World
So long
As I loved you not
The light of yours
Did not find out all the wealth
And the vast sky
With the lamp in his hands was waiting
in the eternal void
Singing did my love come
With what a whisper
She garlanded you with her own garland
Smiling with enamoured eyes
She gave you something in secrecy in your heart secret
And that will remain entangled for ever
Amid the garland of stars.

—Rabindranath Tagore : *Valaka*, *Rabindra-Rachanavali*, Government of West Bengal, Calcutta, 1980, Vol. II, No. 17, p. 463.

[Translated by me]

The association of love in the form of a song with divinity is an altogether new perspective of Tagore's quest for beauty. It brings forth for him a sense of humble dedication. It also marks a note of happy optimism that makes the Poet rather frank and buoyant. As he openly states :

This is good today that I have in this rivers
of unison of laughter and tears
Embraced waves, dived, filled in the bowl of life
and bid farewell
This, then, is good : to sing with this tongue and
to awake in light with flowers
To remain in slumber at midnight with stars
in the hope of a new life.

—Rabindranath Tagore : "Sesh Gaan" ("The Last Song") *Palataka* (*The Runaway*), *Rabindra-Rachanavali*, Government of West Bengal, Calcutta, 1980, Vol. II, p. 537.

[Translated by me]

Even emanicipation takes a nurturing turn in the Poet's quest for beauty. Unlike his intentions to be in slumber with stars at midnight, the Poet makes a delve into the mystery of emancipation from the standpoint of creative beauty :

With manifold images Freedom comes to many a person
And not with a single one.
The wine of fulness flows from world to world
in various tastes and diverse currents
Where my creation Singles with the Creator. I am
there unbounded.
Freedom responds to me in the midst of
music mine.

—Rabindranath Tagore : "*Mukti*" ("Freedom"), *Puravi*, *Rabindra-Rachanavali*, Government of West Bengal, Calcutta, 1980, Vol. II, pp. 641-642.

[Translated by me]

The Poet cannot but respond to the beckoning of the Eternal Dancer in his quest for beauty. The exposition made by him is thrilling :

The Eternal Dancer dances
in the flower in spring,

in the harvest in autumn,
in thy limits, my child,
in thy thoughts and dreams

—Rabindranath Tagore : "*Lekhan*", *Rabindra Rachanavali*, Government of West Bengal, Calcutta, 1980, Vol. II, P. 746.

[Translated by the Poet]

A new concept of beauty emerges from the Poet's vast experience of Nature. The 'sweet incompleteness' of Nature is the infinite charm of human life continually seeking beauty in fulfilment. As the Poet makes an epigrammatic statement :

Beauty smiles in the confinement of the bud
in the heart of a sweet incompleteness.

—Rabindranath Tagore : *Lekhan*, *Rabindra Rachanavali*, Government of West Bengal, Calcutta, 1980, Vol. II, p. 744.

[Translated by the Poet]

Already, the Poet is quite convinced of the mutual relationship between Truth and Beauty. This has added for him an advantage to unfold beauty that merges in the not-yet, and, as it merges in the not-yet the quest becomes unending but adventurous, uncompromising but promising. In his own words,

Truth loves its limits,
for there she meets the beautiful.

—*Ibid.*, p. 745.

[Translated by the Poet]

In his quest for beauty, the Poet sometimes enjoys his vacant mood like the 'derelict clouds' of the sky but even then beauty emerges with extraordinary brilliance of colours. As he elucidates,

I decorate with futile fancies my idle moments
and see them float away in the air
like derelict clouds with their cargo of colours
drifting from somewhere to no destination.

—Rabindranath Tagore : *Lekhan*, *Rabindra-Rachanavali*, Government of West Bengal, Calcutta, 1980, p. 757.

[Translated by the Poet]

Ever alert in the laughter of creation, the Poet goes out in his quest for beauty in the freedom of the wind and the sky, the birds and the streams. Even dumb hours of darkness as he introspects, find language in the stillness of eternity. The quest becomes more entertaining as he plunges into the deep sea of beauty :

Let me not grope in vain in the dark
but keep my mind still in the faith
that the day will break
and truth will appear in the majesty
of its simplicity.

—*Ibid.*, p. 763.
[Translated by the Poet]

Beauty bathed in tears of sorrow is what the Poet craves for. He is ready to embrace sorrow to be christened in the halo of brilliance. The freedom from all encumbrances and constraints as he pines for, becomes a reality :

O Beautiful, you have brought tears
welled up in eyes.
You have brought amid your breast
the fire of penance unbearable.
And so sorrow shines in brilliance
The bonds of life enamoured are torn apart
With this heat does pulsate in efflorescence
the lotus of incoherence.

—Rabindranath Tagore : "*Asru*" ("Tears"), *Mahua*, *Rabindra-Rachanavali*, Government of West Bengal, Calcutta, 1980, Vol. II, p. 841.
[Translated by me]

What should then be the creative ideal in our quest for beauty ? Tagore has a very categorical answer :

In everyday life our personality moves in a narrow circle of immediate self-interest. And therefore our feelings and events, within that short range, become prominent subjects for ourselves. In their vehement self-assertion they ignore their unity with the All. They rise up like obstructions and obscure their own background. But art gives our personality the disinterested freedom of the eternal, there to find it in its true perspective. To see our own home in flames is not to see fire in its verity. But the fire in the stars is the fire in the heart of the Infinite; there, it is the script of creation.

—Rabindranath Tagore : "The Creative Ideal", *Creative Unity*, Macmillan & Co. Limited, London, 1962, p. 39.

The creative ideal, as the Poet elucidates, takes its form in the innermost poignance of creativity and therein lies the brilliance of his quest for beauty. He, therefore, seeks beauty anywhere and everywhere, but the process of seeking every time appears anew with changing processes of imagination. The experimentations with prose-poems point towards their changeability of ideas and expression in search of beauty. The Poet's finer sensibilities in exploring new frontiers of beauty—find a new avenue of manifestation when he toys with lovely imagery-patterns like the runaway boy from the school clasping the ducklings in his breast and spending the whole afternoon beside the pond while the newly wed bride writes letters, tears and writes again :

Amid that interval I see
The runaway boy is playing
        Beside the pond
        With ducklings enclasped in his breast
The whole afternoon shows the boy
        Seated on the landings of the pond alone
Within that gap do I see
        The newly wed bride is writing letters
        Tearing them and writing again
A little bit of smile shines on my face
A little bit of breath also falls.

—Rabindranath Tagore: "*Phank*", ("The Gap"), *Punascha*, *Rabindra-Rachanavali*, Government of West Bengal, Calcutta, 1980, Vol. III, p. 21.

[Translated by me]

In the process of discovering beauty the Poet plays with imageries as freely and abundantly as possible. He allows them to be adorned with the ornaments of his language, the twists and turns appearing as sparklers that dazzle with all lustre. Here is a sudden jolt in the beginning :

It is like a diamond in the middle of the ring
made of platinum
The clouds encompassing the horizon of the sky.
With the midway gap the field flashes with sunlight
Terrific blows the wind
Terror-stricken are the *Papaiya* plants
Rebellion starts in the northern field among the *neem* trees
A sea of scolding sweeps over the heads of the palm trees

—Rabindranath Tagore : "*Sundar*" ("The Beautiful") *Punascha*, *Rabindra-Rachanavali*, Government of West Bengal, Calcutta, 1980, Vol. III, p. 25.
[Translated by me]

The bell of reality rings all on a sudden in the Poet's ears. He becomes rather prosaic and beauty takes a different hue :

Now it is 2-30 p.m.
The shining noon of the drenched forest
Thro' the windows of the north and the south has come
And has engulfed my whole mind.
Know not I why it so appears
Like a day of yonder time is this day.

—*Ibid.*, p. 25.
[Translated by me].

The Poet has intimate acquaintance with this day. He depicts it in a galaxy of imageries beautiful and serene :

No obligation does the day allow
No emergency does it admit
This is a day whizzed away from the anchor of the present
and sailing away
Like a mirage of the past am I seeing it

Was that past ever remained any time, anywhere
Was it not past of the eternal era ?

—*Ibid.*, p. 25.
[Translated by me]

Finally, with the exquisite blend of a series of similes, the Poet enjoys the beauty of the day like the *aalap* in *Goursarang* that touches a mellow sense of melancholy in the strings of the mind :

The beloved seems to me to be known beyond birth—
A time when the heaven or the golden era
or any other era remains out of reach
Likewise this day of *Asad*
Lazy with intoxications of recess
And weaved with the gold and the pearl,
with the shadow and the light
Is bewildered by spreading her covering over the field
In grandeur, too, appears to be there and yet it is not there.
In the *Akashveena* it is like the *aalap* in *Goursarang*
That *aalap* is coming from the backdrop of all times.

—*Ibid.*, p. 25
[Translated by me]

Meanwhile, the *aalap* of the Poet in quest of beauty goes on from time immemorial.

Do we listen to that eternal *aalap* ?

TAGORE'S POETIC VISION IN *CONVALESCENCE* (*AROGYA*)

Written between November 25, 1940 and February 16, 1941, the poems of Rabindranath Tagore's *Convalescence* (*Arogya*) symbolize his maturest poetic vision. Here the Poet is at his best in exposing the fundamental principles of his poetic faith in a very categorical but sombre approach that is pregnant with chiselled thoughts and controlled emotions. The gifts of Truth that he has received throughout his life with joy and sorrow, pleasure and pain have brought forth for him the pleasant memories running riot in poignance in the dust of the earth whom he salutes with sincere reverence. He, therefore, does not for a moment hesitate to recall his gratitude through his poetic vision :

Pleasant is this heaven, pleasant is the earth's dust.
Upon my heart have I recast
This great vow
The message of life did bestow.
Day by day the gifts of truth did I receive whatsoever
Decay in the pleasant juicy form will ne'er favour
This message of vow on the edge of death so rings,
The joy of the endless makes all loss futile and swings.
When I shall depart with the last touch of the earth
I shall say the dust from my path
Has adorned my forehead
The halo of the Eternal have I seen in the mystery of
dismay shrouded

The joyous form of Truth in this dust has taken the image,
Knowing this, I salute the dust on the earth's stage.

—Rabindranath Tagore : *Convalescence (Arogya)*, *Rabindra-Rachanavali*, Government of West Bengal, Calcutta, 1980. Vol. III, No. 1, p. 821.

[Translated by me]

Like a great visionary, the Poet prepares himself for the last journey by adorning himself with the halo of the Eternal whom he had seen shrouded in the mystery of dismay. He claims—and rightly does so—to have entered into the kingdom of endless joy that makes loss futile. The gifts of Truth that he receives and enjoys are the Eternal gifts that make life precious and meaningful. He does not, therefore, want to be disturbed in his preparation for the final farewell to this endearing earth :

Oft do I think as if the time for adieu has come
Cast the veil on the day of farewell
Of the light of the controlled setting sun
Let the parting time
Be peaceful and silent, let not the assembly of condolence
Create the illusion of bereavement.

—*Ibid.*, No. 31, p. 839.
[Translated by me]

Is the Poet waiting to see the grand assembly of the seven saints of heaven ? The halo is already there. Let peace come down on earth. He has seen the assembly of leaves proclaiming the message of peace. And so, he prays :

Let the rows of forest at the door of departure
Proclaims the message of peace of the world with the assembly of leaves
Let the silent blessings of the night—
The offerings of the halo of seven saints—
Come down.

—*Ibid.*, No. 31, p. 839.
[Translated by me]

Looking contented and pleased at himself he recalls how he is blessed with the touch of greatest men and honoured with the gifts of God, specially with the 'sweet blessings of beauty' that allow him to see and know his own self. As he admits :

The sweet blessings of beauty have I received in this life,
In the hemlock of human love do I receive the taste of pipe.
In unbearable sorrowful days
Known have I the self that unhurt and unbeaten stays.

—*Ibid.*, No. 29, p. 838.
[Translated by me]

How does the Poet feel when the vision of death appears to him in the form of a shadow ?

The day when I have felt the shadow of death in sight
I faced not defeat meek at the hands of fright.

—*Ibid.*, No. 29, p. 838.
[Translated by me]

The reason is not far to seek, for the Poet is ever favoured with the association of greatest personalities :

Ne'er was I from the touch of the greatest men debarred
Their message of nectar in the heart I have treasured.
The honour of the God of life that I've received in the life of mine
With grateful mind that memorandum do I entwine.

—*Ibid.*, No. 29, p. 838.
[Translated by me]

Of course, with the waning of days, the Poet is rather contemptative in his tone and temperament. The imminent hours of farewell make him terribly conscious. Does he want to evaluate the present seen through the mirror of the past ? Is the sense of desolation an overpowering factor in the vision of the past ? Here is the Poet's confession :

Day after day wanes away, silently I remain seated,
Thinking over the gifts of life how much is left
By meeting the wastage of savings.
What is waned *sans* care,
Whate'er due I have received, whate'er to be given I've delivered
What is left as the remnant for the end.
Those who came near, those who went far away
With what tunings of mine their touch has still remained
Whom I recognized not in absent mindedness.
The footfalls of farewell today are ringing in the heart in vain
Perhaps I knew not who had left away forgiving me
Without speaking.

—*Ibid.*, No. 16, p. 832.
[Translated by me]

Fully aware of his own limitations, the Poet begs to be excused of his errors and wants his love for one and all to remain unalloyed even at the cost of his life. The strappings of life are to be renewed, if necessary, with the price of death :

If any error do I commit, its judgment
Will you in grievance nurse when I shall be no more ?
So many ties were torn, the strappings of life
No time will find to be entwined.
The Love that has continually remained at the fag end of life,
If any sign of wound is inflicted with any dishonour of mine
Let healing be brought forth with my palms of death :
This do I speak time and again.

—*Ibid.*, No. 16, p. 831.
[Translated by me]

The joy of poetic fulfilment as the Poet visualizes at the fag end of his life is symbolized in the brightness of *Palash*—a flower of vibrant spring or the youth of life. Quite conscious of his scant role in the feast of living affluence, the note of melancholy strains rings in agonizing words of muse :

Palash is the emblem of joy of the spring of life,
Today to one bereft of honour
In his poor hours you met
Where I, the companionless, am alone
Out of the courtyard of ceremonies
On the sandy shores of the desert *sans* crops.
Where from the boisterous garden of life of this earth
My unwelcome days towards streams lost
Like torn sheets are gone afloating
At the end of the spring.
—*Ibid.*, No. 11, p. 829.

[Translated by me]

But optimistic as the Poet is, he still receives the warm welcome of the Beautiful. The waning days turn brilliant in the resonance of youth. He re-lives in the vision of the reception of the gifts of the All Beautiful. The words of gratitude, therefore, come out in spontaneity :

Even then, your gift is beyond austerity
The full price of youth you have offered in my heart *sans* lustre.
The aversion of Providence you denied not
Her tiredness you did ameliorate,
Conveyed me and so am I all the time
Prized with the welcome of Beauty, the invitation of the young.

—*Ibid.*, No. 11, p. 829.
[Translated by me]

Sorrow takes a different turn in the Poet's vision of the All Beautiful. The splashed light of joy that has made thrilling inroads to his creative sensibilities has, indeed, eliminated all darkness and the slogan of victory from the inherent source of life pulsates him with ever nourishing strength of optimism :

The door of the mind was open, suddenly in unawareness
The stroke of sorrow befell there I know not from where
The shame gushed forth the unexposed strength
That embodies the inherent source of life
The slogan of victory from above
Instantly came down in the mind thro' the path of the horizon
The splashed light of joy
Spread in a moment in the mind, piercing the cloud of darkness.

—*Ibid.*, No. 12, p. 829.
[Translated by me]

The ceremony of joy in which the Poet wants to participate with full-throated ease paves its boundless way in his mind allowing it to be a joyous partner in spontaneity. As a consequence, the clamours of sorrow are transformed into shadows. With the victory of joy the Poet celebrates the march of beyonding :

The humiliation of the tiny crevice
Was abolished, saw I my place in the seat of the world.
With joy in abundance
My mind embraced victory.
The avenue of ceremony
In glory did identify its own world in the arena of emancipation.
The clamours arising out of sorrow
Turned into shadows and ematiated in it.

—*Ibid.*, No. 12, p. 829.
[Translated by me]

The Poet contemplates on the edge of the open window the beckoning of the world living and dynamic. The sense of appreciation gets a new image in the excellence of language :

On the edge of the open window in the distant room
I remain seated on the dumb tomb
Outside, in the rhythm of the green songs herald
The beckonings of the light of the world

Towards the flow of the origin of eternity
Thc mind floats on with the horizon's bluish spree
To whom adoration is to be sent
Is the eager mind's only incumbent.
On he seeks in the image of words the priceless to pay,
Not a word does he say.
Glad am I, he murmurs, rhythm comes to a stop,
Says he, the harvest of thanks I crop.

—*Ibid.*, No. 5, p. 825.
[Translated by me]

The gladness in the Poet's mind is nourished in endless beauty even during departing years. He is enjoying the workless idle time in the unending needle fight to adroitly sew the best possible piece of Nature. In sincere artistry, with the swarm of crickets dazzling trees in abundance, the meaningless nothing enjoys harmony in the void of his life. As he says :

Sewing the sparklers amid the veil of rhythm
The workless idle time is in the work of needle fight filled.
The meaningless nothing in eyes dazzles
The rhyme enjoys harmony in blanks
The swarm of crickets on trees
Dazzle;
That is not the flame of the lamp, in darkness the night plays.
Sewing beads of light.

—*Ibid.*, No. 28, p. 838.
[Translated by me]

The Poet knows well that the beads of light sewn by darkness is the perfume of promise of his own life. In his inward vision the intertwining of work and play proves the point that there is an uninterrupted onward march in creation. And so he is emboldened with the creative spree of his mind—its vastness beckons the spring of his life with renewed spirit of freshness :

The little flowers in the trees of the meadows awake
That does not a garden create, dots of colour adorn the grass.
It arrests the mind useful as well in hundreds it spreads in the world
Not, of course, to be recalled, it, too, does spread in legion
The water of the spring runs to make the soil fertile
The foams puff up and shatter just afterwards
Work and play are intertwined
The burden is eased for that, and the Lord of creation is pleased.

—*Ibid.*, No. 28, p. 838.
[Translated by me]

In the evening of life, the Poet visualizes the role of fame in his life set against disgrace and authority that continually serve as agents of consciousness. He knows well that there are some appreciators for whom he has done very little in response to their untiring devotion, and so he evaluates himself :

Crossing over fame and disgrace have I arrived at the evening of life
Seated on the steps of adieu
Doubtlessly have I believed this physique of my own,
With the chance of disease it does mock at itself
See I in every activity it brings forth a disaster,
My authority does disown.
To save from that disgrace
Those who untiringly guard
Have stood beside me in the last welcome of the end of the day
Let me not disclose their names, let them remain in the mind
They've given me the last recognition of good fortune,
They've made me forget the defeat of the frail heart
They admit
Fame and authority to the befitting and to the able belong.

—*Ibid.*, No. 15, p. 831.
[Translated by me]

The Poet is christened with a great vision of truth :

The lot of the unable
the best gift does await.

—*Ibid.*, No. 15, p. 831.
[Translated by me]

Conversely, he is also christened with the truth arrived at the end of diverse experiences that one is to pay the price of one's fame thoughout one's life :

All through the life the price of fame is to be paid
No wastage does it allow,

—*Ibid.*, No. 15, p. 831.
[Translated by me]

and the offerings of love that make an end to poverty are only a beginning to welcome poverty again :

With the end of all poverty the offerings of love
does that poverty bring back.

—*Ibid.*, No. 15, p. 831.
[Translated by me]

but the Poet, like a great visionary, foresees the sign of the illuminating endless :

The sign of the endless dazzles there.

—*Ibid.*, No. 15 p. 831.
[Translated by me]

The untold words as the Poet visualizes have received a sudden jolt to be freed from the humdrum affairs of life and to be partners in his poetic creation. He also foresees them as a cluster of stars in the vast sky of his creation. As he observes :

In the vast human mind
The cluster of words untold
Comes back from time to time with emotions unexpressed
Like stars in the enormous oblivion.
In the arena of my mind

Suddenly being whisked away in a stroke
Consolidated has it become
And is rotating in my creative hemisphere.

—*Ibid.*, No. 25, p. 836.
[Translated by me]

Even from his ailing bed, the Poet cannot but make an intimate relationship with the day to day affairs of life. The wintry noon glides lazily like the mossy currents of a stream and the Poet finds a point of similarity with his idle moments of the declining years of his life. What a calm acceptance of the sudden turn of life hectic, busy and brisk !

The lonely room of the patient
Thro' open windows
The curved shadow lies prostrated on the bed
The drowsy hours of winter with the heat of noon
Slowly trek on
Like the mossy current of a river,
Oft, as if, permeates the sigh of the distant past
In cropless fields.

—*Ibid*, No. 3, p. 822.
[Translated by me]

The glorious boyhood days appear like a thrillingly vivid picture in the canvas of the Poet's mind. The fishing boats, the sparkling pitchers adorning the village girls, the humming zigzag avenues, companionless white clouds—all create an intense nostalgic feeling of winter :

I remember how long
The *Padma* under the broken banks
In shade and light
Of jobless middle-aged morning
Does make my aimless thoughts floating
In foams and foams.
Touching the edge of the oblivion
The fishing boats go a-sailing
In the corner of the sky does lie the white cloud
companionless.

In sparkling pitchers on the waists of rural girls
In their closeted conversations under head-coverings
In humming zigzag avenues under the shadow of
mango-groves
The cuckoo coos at times in lone branches, O where,
The rural mode of life ashamed of shade
Trembles on the veil of mystery in my mind.
The pond-sides puff up with crops of mustard seedlings
The gift of the sun with the earth's return,
The flowery offerings are placed at the temple of the sun.

—*Ibid.*, No. 3, p. 822.
[Translated by me]

Does this nostalgia end in itself ? The Poet has an inward vision. It is the vision of his own imperfection expressed in his silent invocation. In the fading blue of the autumn sky at noon the Poet's message mingles :

In lonely hours do I spread my quiet sight
I have sent my silent salutation
To the sun with whose light the first man
On the altar of the earth has seen the image of God.
I've thought aside
If the message of the vedic hymn of the past
My voice would adorn,
The chanting of mine would in this light unite
No language do I have, no language, indeed;
Looking at the distant horizon
I've spread my silence in the faded blue of
the sky at noon.

—*Ibid.*, No. 3, pp. 822-23.
[Translated by me]

In a lighter vein, the Poet compares himself with jobless persons and finds himself in a very entertaining mood because he is now indifferent to time and greatly fears persons who are time-conscious :

Eternally am I in the group of the jobless;

In trash writing and reading, my days roll on
in sham strategies,
I welcome the learned who spends his time in
unwanted mood
With care in my sitting room saying 'come, please come'.
I do fear the work-worried people
Tightly they have arrested time with watches
in their wrists
Nothing is there to spend in extravagance to an excess
Idle folk like us are ashamed of this amid them.
Masters are we to idle away time
To disrupt work in manifold ways, we lay our traps
This frame of mine does keep the busy far away
Strength have I not to surcharge others' frames.

—*Ibid.*, No. 21, p. 834.
[Translated by me]

But, then, the Poet has a deep sense of gratitude. He cannot but gratefully remember the untiring devotion to service by "Sarojdada" at his own sweet will. Sometimes the idea of the messenger of God in the form of the latter peeps in the Poet's mind. And suddenly he becomes rather sombre in his failure to be so endearing and self-forgetful as "Sarojdada" is. What a grace of God to receive his companionship in the service of the so-called time-shy, workless person like "Sarojdada" !

I look at Sarojdada
He agrees at everything as if he has no work
Unlocked is the storehouse of his time,
The demands of the disabled like me
Enjoy leisure from him wide and uninterrupted
Bounteous, untiring and dependable,
At dead night in drooping light
Suddenly his image my eyes visualize
Think I aside, who sent the messenger rowing the
boat of assurance
The nightmare of adversaries did erase

This unimagined debut of a man *sans* any assignment
Is a priceless profit in the prison-house of merciless
providence.

—*Ibid.*, No. 21, p. 834.
[Translated by me]

Does the Poet see his second childhood through his ailing health ? Is he, like a child, craving for affection and love ? As he introspects,

When this body with decay and disease
Strength does lose day by day
Youth slips away leaving this tattered nest
Childhood alone remains
In the closed room outside the world of action-grieved
one
The frail mind of the child its mother haunts.
The heart *sans* wealth is allured
The shelter of affection without price
To receive from someone
Whose debut
To the shortlived does offer
The first honour of life.

—*Ibid.*, No. 17, p. 832.
[Translated by me]

The first honour that the Poet as a debutant intends to receive peeps through the splendour of the evening in the fading moments of his life. The grandeur of darkness and light that salutes silence brings forth for him a deep moment of devotion to Eternity—to the last journey by sea unending. As he portrays the serene picture of evening in the canvas of Truth :

Slowly comes the evening, all the strings loosen
one by one
From the web of hours. The day did sacrifice
Opening the lion-marked western gate
All its golden grandeur
In the marriage of darkness and light

Salutes in silence bending towards the distant east
Slowly closes its eyes down, the time has come
The apparent identity in meditation deep
To be delved.
Where the infinite sky the sphere of blessings of the stars
Covers up the formless existence of the beauty of the day
Truth to be attained there itself
Oars on in the sea of night.

—*Ibid.*, No. 30, pp. 838-839.
[Translated by me]

The Poet's journey for truth oaring the sea of night invigorates him to express love in a new pattern through reminiscence. The boisterous role of love in youthful days even now peeps in the mind with all vividness :

Love came once in young age
With murmurs of the fountain.
From the peak unknown
With a sudden sense of wonder
The static direction of stones curved like eyebrows
Being carried over with overflowing frown
Making the wind restless
Waving amid the flow of identity
The language of unimaginable mystery of the unknown
All around whatever is static, proportionate and eternally exposed
The flow of running revolt rings with the muse of emancipation.

—*Ibid.*, No. 13, pp. 829-833.
[Translated by me]

And what about the role of that boisterous youth today ?

What about the running revolt of love ? Silence, serenity sombreness, peace, and the saintly night—all have replaced youth and love :

That love today with the silence of pleasing consolation
In the backdrop of the deep has remained soundless.

Everywhere in the vastness of peace of the world
It is in unassuming unison
Its light is with the light of the stars of the meditating night
Its beauty is with the flowery offerings of worship of the night.

—*Ibid.*, No. 13, p. 830.
[Translated by me]

The beauty of the earth with all 'flowery offerings of worship' appeals the Poet's mind. The sense of wonder that the Mother Earth creates has a deep attraction for him. She appears with her new dress :

This much is the askance with the 'let-you-remain' mind.
Who can convey the demand of the world to Him
Only to live ?
Again and again this wonder
Arrives at the heart
With the profound call of the world blessed with life
Mother comes and stands—
The mother ever old—with the dress of the new.

Ibid., No. 17, p. 832.
[Translated by me]

The newness of the dress of the Mother Earth cannot be left aside in oblivion. The Poet has a deep sense of gratitude for her. The 'pale fine firmament', the forest with stretched out arms, the young sun with the scarf of transparent light—all have their glowing place in the canvas of the Poet's mind. As he writes :

The pale fine firmament is in the great distance
The forest stretches its long arm overhead beneath her
And silently does submit its own green offerings.
The young sun of *Magh* on earth.
Spreads everywhere the scarf of transparent light.
This had I put in writing
Ere the stoical artist erased this picture.

Ibid., No. 6, p. 825.
[Translated by me]

The slow life on the idle bed that the Poet passes weaves art even in the mossy shed. A renewed view of honour flashes out in humility. As the Poet observes :

Slowly goes life beside the idle bed.
Artistry does create in the mossy shed
No honour it has, yet it remains there, too.
The little worth of life, identities a few.

—*Ibid.*, No. 84, p. 836.
[Translated by me]

The idle moments of the Poet's life do not go unrewarded. The king of mountains, as he thinks, sends juicy containers for him in bright sunlight. The 'liaison of the refreshing heart' comes closer to the murmurings of the profound forest groves to be his partner. His acknowledgement of friendship is made by his 'disease-dubbed pen' in words of blessings :

The juiceful containers of
The distant lemon-garden of the king of mountains
Brought at the feet of this bed
The friendship of the sun of the lovely morning
The golden writings
Of the spray of light splashed
Entangled with soundless murmurings
Of profound forest-groves
The liaison of the refreshing heart remains.
With the beckonings of the rare language of the disease-dubbed pen
The Poet conveys his blessings.

—*Ibid.*, No. 22, p. 835.
[Translated by me]

With the shame of defeat and boredom from which the Poet terribly suffers, the beckoning of the golden flag brings a new aura of hope. Darkness goes away with the pleasing light of the morning sun. The promise of life is reassured. The Poet visualizes the defeat of sorrow within himself from an altogether renewed perspective of life. The arrival of the night of life is dramatically portrayed :

Silently comes the ferocious night,
Breaking the flexible bars of body *sans* strength
Enters the heart
Goes on stealing the glorious *mien* of life.

—*Ibid.*, No. 7, p. 826.
[Translated by me]

How does the mind of the Poet react ?
The mind does accept defeat at the hands of humiliation.
When the shame of this defeat, the disgrace of boredom
Darkens, suddenly in the horizon is seen
The flag of the day painted with the light of gold
From the distant centre what a sound, as it were,
Arises to declare it false.

—*Ibid.*, No. 7, p. 826.
[Translated by me]

And just then, in the pleasing morning light, the Poet visualizes the flag of victory atop the fort of his frail body :

In the pleasing light of the morn
I behold the image of myself, the winner of sorrow
On the peak of the fort of the worn out body.

—*Ibid.*, No. 7, p. 826.
[Translated by me]

Elsewhere, the Poet is in full-throated voice of appreciation with his incomparable imagery-patterns woven in all fireflies of artistry :

The most beautiful
Is adorned in the holy morning
Of the bathing of light
The unending formless
With the touchstone of infinite forms
Is creating images of appreciation,
Everyday
The welome of the ever new
At the altar of the ever old.

With unison of the green and the blue firmament
The scarf of the earth
In light and shade goes a-weaving
The hearbeat of the sky
Does throb from leaf to leaf
The morning's necklace sparkles
From forest to forest
The unaccountable songs of birds
Go on thanking the goddess the affluence of life
The touch of human love
Does bring forth the meaning of nectar in fusion with all,
Turns the dust of the earth pleasant.
And spreads the throne for the Eternal Man everywhere.

—*Ibid.*, No. 2, pp. 821-822.
[Translated by me]

The neglected pictures of the Poet's early life revive again. Like Wordsworth, he is also haunted by their living memories. Here is an excellent sketch—a living drama of human life that aches the waning heart lost in the melee of a sudden void, but that is so sweet in breath-taking beauty of nostalgia :

At a distance, the bell rings
The clamorous self-announcement piercing the sky of the town
From the mind disappeared
In the heated sun of *Magh*, flashed in the eyes without reason the picture
That on the edge of the way of life not very visible remained,
Knitting the hamlets the meadowy path has towards the distance gone
Crossing o'er the embankments of the river
The ancient shade of the *Asatha* tree,
The people are seated in the hope of crossing the river
Keeping the marketing products nearby.
In the tinplate rooms of the *gunge*
Files of pitchers with condensed juice of sugar-candies.
The dogs of the locality lick by being a prey to perfume.

Flies crowd.
On the roads, carts put upside down
Are burdened with jute
Weighing goes on aloud by pulling the bags one by one.
In the courtyard of the storehouse.
The oxen bereft of yokes
Squander on the green edge of the road by eating grass,
Beat on the back by hairy fan of the tail
Heaps of mustard are there
Waiting for storage in the corn-containers.
The fishing boats come on the banks,
The fisherwomen have assembled with buckets on their waists :
Overhead the kite flies.
The business-boats are bound side by side on the sloping sandbanks.
Sitting in the sun, the oarsmen are weaving nets on the roof of tin sheds
The ploughman floats on swimming by clasping the neck of the buffalo
Towards the other side in paddy fields.
Beyond the forest, the apex of the temple not far away
Is shining in the morning sunlight.
Beyond the visible side of the field the train runs on
With gradually feeble
Whistling lines of sound drawn on the canvas of ether
Spreading the smoke behind.
As a mark of the long flag of victory of winning the distance

I remember, that's nothing, long long ago,
It was midnight.
The boats were anchored on the bank of the Ganges
The shining water in moonlight.
The images of shadow consolidated on the edges of the forest untrembled

The flame of the lamp is rarely seen thro' the forest.
Suddenly I awoke
In the soundless midnight sky

The young voice in the song echoes,
The lean boat sweepingly runs in the ebb-tide current
In an instant it vanished :
Mystery reigned in the sombre forest on the two banks :
The image of the quiet night dressed with the crown of the moon
In the seat of the humbled slumber did speechless remain.
The western bank of the Ganges, the residence is at the fag end of the town
The long stretched sand bank
Beneath the vacant sky as if makes a commentary on futility
Cows graze to and fro in the empty field of maize
From the creepers of water-melon
The farmer-boy drives with a stick the goats away
Somewhere, again the rural woman
Roams in search of spinach with basket on her waist.
Oft beside river-line far away
A group of oarsmen with bowed down backs, tired movements, pulling the ropes.
No more freshness prevails in the water or land all day long.
In the nearby garden, the *golakchanpa* is unendeared
The old great *neem* tree with seat prepared below
The aristocratic shadow of hers deep and serene.
Storks bake shelter at night there.
The water pulled out of the well
All day long makes rippling sounds in its course through the drains

To instil life in the fields of oats.
Bhajiya crushes wheat in a wheel-crusher
With her brass-bangled hands
The stretched tune the noon enchants.

This on-the-way scene
Transitorv as it was
In the distant domain of consciousness,
Up that comes in the mind today,
All these pictures discarded

The latest pain of separation of life
Bring foıth in the mind with the sound of the distant bell.

—*Ibid.*, No. 4, pp. 823-825.
[Translated by me]

A historic panorama of life casts a definite spell upon the Poet's mind. He delves deep into the historic past of India and flashes the pearls of the past happenings before our eyes :

Rowing through the flow of idle time
The mind goes on looking towards emptiness
The picture painted in shadow arrests the eyes in the
path of that vast emptiness
In groups, for time endless, so many people have gone
In time long past
In forceful speed of the pomp of victory.
The groups of the Pathans have come with the
greed of empire.
The Moghuls have come.
The wheels of the chariot of victory.
Have sped past the web of dust and the flag of victory
Towards the avenue of emptiness do I look
No trace of that do I find today.
In that clear sky in the morn and in the eve
The light of sunrise and sunset adorned from
time to time.
Once again in that abode of emptiness
In groups have come
Thro' iron-string avenue
In the chariot that believes in fire
The mighty English
Have exposed their power.
Know I that time would flow on even in their avenue
To the endless would it sweep away the countrywide
dragnet of empire.
Know I that her soldiers carrying the burden of
commodities.
Would leave no trace in the avenue of the world of light.
Opening eyes towards the world of earth

We see there in murmuring sounds
Endless crowd tread on
In diverse avenues and in different groups
From time beyond time in eternal human needs
In life and in death.

—*Ibid.*, No. 10, pp. 827-828.
[Translated by me]

How does the Poet expose the day to day activities of the people who work hard and the worries and anxieties from which they continually suffer ? How done he expose their sounds of great chanting of life ? Here is a living document in the serene words of poetry :

Endlessly do they
Pull on oars, hold on the steering,
From field to field do they
Sow seeds, reap ripe paddy.
They work
In cities and fields.
The septre tumbles down, no sound emerges from the drum of war,
The tower of victory forgets like the dunce its meaning
All the bloody eyes with bloodstained weapons in hands
Remain wrapped in stories meant for children
They work
In countries beyond countries
In the sea-shores and river-banks of *Anga*, *Banga* and *Kalinga*,
In Punjab, Bombay and Gujarat.
The roaring and the humming sounds
By day and at night are enclasped and make the passing of the day enamoured.
Sorrow and happiness, day and night
The sounds of great chanting of life do make resonant.
On the remains of ruins of hundreds of empires
They work.

—*Ibid.*, No. 10, p. 828
[Translated by me]

Side by side with the exposure of human endeavour for progress of humanity, the Poet also makes an introspective analysis of the dumb language of his devoted dog who remains seated by his side silently and acknowledges his affection with a thrilling sense of emotion :

Amid the speechless world of animals
This creature alone
Barring all good and evil.
The man *in toto* has seen.
It has seen one to whom in joy the life can be laid
Love uncalled for can be showered upon,
To the unending world of consciousness,
One whose awareness the avenue shows.
When I behold the dumb heart's
Untiring self-submission
Proclaiming the poverty of its own,
I fail to make out what price it has haunted out
With its easy feelings in the form of man.
The piteous anxieties of its speechless look
Fails to spell out whatever it feels,
It makes me understand : The real worth of man is
in the creation.

—*Ibid.*, No. 14, p. 830.
[Translated by me]

It might occur to some one why the Poet veers from one idea to the other like the wings of a compass. In response to this, the Poet has a definite say :

In the vast human mind
The cluster of words untold
Hovers from time to time with emotions unexpressed
Like a nebula in the enormous oblivion.
In the arena of my mind
Suddenly being whisked away in a stroke
Consolidated has it become
And is rotating in my creative hemisphere.

—*Ibid.*, No. 25, p. 836.
[Translated by me]

Looking within himself, the Poet feels rather desolate for his failure to reap the best harvest in his life. But he hopes that in the dying month of life, he might remain associated with the world with all its freshness by having his permanent place in the shadow of the wild bush :

With the reaping of harvest, the cornfield becomes vacant
The crop of neglect, spinach, grows of value scant.
The women of the poor families come to pluck in plenty
Home they return in joy, whatever they get the bounteous
pretty.
Today I fail to plough, no scope for ploughing have I
In left out cornfields' idleness, lazy days I pass by.
Life in land is somewhat there, the seed is not yet ripe,
Fruit it does not bring forth, the soil is still alive.
My *Sravan* has gone away, there's rain no more
Aghran with golden days of paddy is already o'er.
My *Chaitra* is burnt in the sun, when the river is dry
If under the bush of fruit wild its shadow does sigh
I shall know then that in my last month my lot did not slip,
My enchantment with the green world still does peep.

—*Ibid.*, No. 18, pp. 802-833.
[Translated by me]

With imaginations roaming in his mind as free as a flying bird, the Poet takes accounts of his words recollected in his mind. He finds dreams exceptionally meaningful and surprisingly beautiful. Here is an excellent exposition of the Poet's views on the role of the artist and the function of art :

My mind recollects words here and there
As if the autumnal clouds are roaming after rains
in the air.
Falsly does it travel without the string of work
in the space,
Sometimes it paints in silver, reveals sometimes the
golden colour in grace.
In the corner of the horizon does it build
an image strange,

Again and again it makes in a vacant mind of
lines a change.
That artistry of vapour is as if the neglect of joy,
Nowhere is it responsible, and so it makes the
meaningless game of toy.
Conscious is it to awake and so to be up and
doing in work.
Slumber has nothing to do, and so in distorted dreams
to embark.
The mood of the mind's dream is under the yoke of work.
No holiday does it enjoy in autonomy's park.
With imaginations that crowd in its being free.
Like a flying bird does it build a nest in dream's artistry.
And so feel I the evidence within me
The oldest component of the universe is the dream's
insanity.
The process of creation checks it and perennial does
it make.
With terrible strength does its authority intake.
The skill of art is to arrest this boisterous fly
For the unreachable to have a try.

—*Ibid.*, No. 26, pp. 836-837.
[Translated by me]

To arrest the boisterous fly of dreams in the waning years of his life, makes the Poet very profound in his sensibilities. With his incomparable process of creation, he wants to have a deeper view of life in all its perfection. As a poet, he has the artistic power to weave emotions in words controlled and serene and has also the firm conviction within himself that the meagre contribution to the woıld of literature might leave like lifeless coral some impression despite the fact that many more hidden thoughts remain buried in the disgıace of confidentialities or exposures. A poignant touch of the Poet's inability to adore the unexposed beauty is revealed in a self-conscious vein that merges in the spirit of an autobiography :

The web of rhythm of words that I have learnt to weave
Is trapped there

In the unreachable that avert the eyes of alertness
In the depth of mind unseen.
I want to thwart her in name, but name she does deny.
If any worth she has,
Day by day that worth is revealed,
Passes from hand to hand.
If with sudden recognition her surprise
Does entice,
No room she gets in human habitation
For sometime in the shores of the mind she does remain enkindled
Nursed in confidence
In the disgrace of exposure
In sands does unite day by day.
This weariness is deserted and empty in the world of hurry,
The gift of the unknown has left something from age to age
In this great island of the language of literature
Like lifeless coral.

—*Ibid.*, No. 27, p. 837.
[Translated by me]

A life-long seeker of Light Eternal, the Poet introspects on his farewell to earth and journey to 'the peak of the last pilgrim-temple'. A foreseer of the end or the beginning of life, he reads the language of the infinite in the horizon. The beckoning of fulness reaches his ears, and so he speaks out :

Sitting alone beside the edged window of the world
The eyes encounter the language of the endless in the horizon of the sky.
Embraced in shadow does the light come
Carrying the smooth friendship of the green from the *Sirish* tree.
In the mind rings : not far, not very far.
The line of the avenue merged in the backdrop of the peak of the setting mountain,

Silent am I beside the door of the inn of the day's end,
In the distance, at times, lustre spreads
The peak of the last pilgrim-temple.
There at the entrance-door the *raagini* of the day's
end plays on,
With whose resonance whatever is beautiful in this life,
Whatever touches the heart in its long journey
Is merged with beckonings of fulness
In the mind rings : not far, not very far.

—*Ibid.*, No. 8, p. 826
[Translated by me]

As an inseparable part of the Endless, the Poet also wants to be a party to the game of fireworks of creation. In his march towards fulness, he must exhibit his splinter of fire. As he says,

Amid the vast creation
The game of fireworks throughout the sky
Goes on along with the sun and the stars
In the yardstick of age beyond age.
I have also come from the endless and the invisible
With trifling splinter of the fire
At one end in a small space and time.
Come as I have today in the act of departure,
The flame of the lamp turned pale,
The reality of enchantment of this play is revealed
in shadow,
Slowly the dramatic costumes
Of happiness and sorrow become loose.

—*Ibid.*, No. 9, pp. 826-827
[Translated by me]

How does the Poet as a player visualize the *Nataraj*—the King of players ?

I saw : from time to time players in legion
Have left their variegated dresses
Outside the door of the theatre.
I saw :

In the 'drop of hundreds of switched-off stars
The silent and lone *Nataraj.*

—*Ibid.*, No. 9, p. 827.
[Translated by me]

With the mark of victory on his forehead, the Poet is now prepared for unison with the Great in the joyous festival of light :

The touch of joy in the heart of light I receive
Know I that my soul no difference does conceive.
From an ancient lustrous source
In the holy current of conscious course
Initiated have I been
On the forehead, the mark of victory was given,
It has informed that the source of nectar I know
With the Great I can unite and glow
In this world of wonder
In the avenue of joy I may enter.

—*Ibid.*, No. 32, p. 839.
[Translated by me]

The great moment for unison with Light, as the Poet thinks, has come right now. Let us join the prayer for the light of joy of the Man Eternal :

Let the cocoon of this life unmask
The bright halo of consciousness
Express the eternal from of Truth
By piercing the mist.
Let the light of joy of a Man Eternal.
Amid all men
Be enkindled in my mind.
Beyond the silent world of wordly grievance
Let me behold the blessed form of the Eternal.
Whatever is amply meaningless and critical in this life,
Whatever embodies falsehood in the sham value of the society,

Leaving aside all beggarly and
Troubled crowd
Let me know the true meaning with my vivid eyes
Prior to crossing the bar.

—*Ibid.*, No. 33, p. 840
[Translated by me]

THE WORLD OF TAGORE'S FOLK SONGS

> One who understands the nature of the Bodhi-hridaya sees everything with a loving heart; for love is the essence of Bodhi-hridaya.
>
> D.T. Joshi : *Outlines of Mahāyāna Buddhism* Quoted by Rabindranath Tagore : "An Indian Folk Religion", *Creative Unity*. Macmillan & Co., Limited, London 1962, p. 75.

Speaking on the characteristics of the folk religion of India, Rabindranath Tagore endeavours to trace the origin of folk culture of India with special reference to the Buddhistic principle of *Bodhi-hridaya*—'the heart of the Eternal Enlightenment' as he quotes the above lines that emphasizes on the role of love in folk imagination and the folk concept of religion. In fact, the statement of Nagarjuna as quoted by Tagore reveals the basic principle of humanity.

The transcendence of man from his individual finite self to the all-embracing infinite self by means of truth arrived at through religion is the fundamental point of interest of Tagore's folk songs. The real fulfilment of the mind is the enlightenment that is achieved by a continual search for Truth. The World of Tagore's folk songs is the world of the embodiment of this Truth through enlightenment where love plays a very important role. He elucidates the point as follows :

> Man would never feel the indignity of his limitations if these were inevitable. Within him he has glimpses of the Infinite, which give him assurance that this truth is not in his limitations, but that this truth can be attained by love. For love is the positive quality of the Infinite, and

love's sacrifice accordingly does not lead to emptiness, but to fulfilment, to *Bodhi-hridaya*, 'the heart of enlightenment'.

—Rabindranath Tagore : "An Indian Folk Religion", *Creative Unity*, Macmillan & Co., London, 1962, p. 75.

The world of Tagore's folk songs is, in fact, the world of love for one and all irrespective of caste, creed, community, colour, religion etc. As an ordinary member of the village community, he extensively travelled Shelaidah (now in Bangladesh) where he came in close contact with the *bauls*. The homeless singing minstrels. The 'Murshida' and 'Marafti' songs of the Muslim devotees have greatly influenced his folk songs. The following folk song has, for instance, deeply influenced him :

Manuse manus viraje
Khoonje neoa vara daay,
Manik chine du ek jane
Se Mahajaner Kripaay

Manus aachhe prati ghate,
Dure nay, ati nikate,
Phooler kali aapni phoote
Bhramar chhute kaachhe jaay.

Man heralds man.
Difficult it is to find out or trace,
The jewel is identified by one or two,
Even that, too, by the Great Man's grace.

Man is existent,
Be it far or very near, at every place,
The flower-bud blooms by itself,
The bee runs forward and embrace,

[Translated by me]

Tagore was also influenced by another folk song that reveals the inner spirit of mankind in a new light of vision :

Jaar tare pran kendechhe
Se to tomar hride aachhe,

Vaaire theke dakchho Kaachhe,
Pavena taare Khoonjchho michhe
Naam dham na jaanle pare
Keman kare dharve taanre
Dekhte saadh hay antare
Thhikaanaa taar sadhur kaachhe

He, for whom your heart aches,
In your heart he does remain,
Whom do you call from outside?
You won't have Him,
Seek ye in vain,
You know not His whereabout.
How, then, would you find Him out?
If the desire to see Him does sprout
His address from the saint you'll gain.
[Translated by me]

During his stay at Shelaidah (now in Bangladesh), Tagore came in contact with such types of saints as stated above. The following reveals a vivid account of the genesis of his love for the Baüls of Bengal :

> Gurudev found a group of lover-devotees as his companions in the rural areas og Shelaidah. They are today famous in the name of Baüls in Bengal. They are a special community. Very few of this community existed till then. Both the Hindus and the Muslims were there in that community. But, in religion, they were neither the Hindus nor the Muslims. Their spiritual life was built on the harmony of these two religions. They are saints of love. They receive enjoyment by loving a special object of love unknown, strange and bereft of physique. They name it "*maner manush*" ("The man of the mind"). Unlike other gods and goddesses, that Man of the mind is not a symbol of any spirit. He does nothing good or bad to man of the real life. He is existent. In secret He is existent in every man. They receive the message of that inherent Man of the mind through meditation of love. But they cannot catch hold of

him. So, in the language of their songs, the unending pain of not knowing that Man of the mind has always been expressed in the language of their songs. The more are they advancing towards the avenue of knowing Him, the more they feel that the distance of not knowing is as if going on increasing. They do not find the signal to its end. The Baüls think that through the pains of non-receiving and unknowing, one finds out that avenue. The mind is filled with the feelings of knowing the unknown through intensity of pains. So they do not aspire after alleviating the sorrow of not knowing the unknown. The meditation of the Baüls of the locality of Shelaidah is one of such a mixture of sorrow and joy closely related to love which does not necessitate any extrinsic support. When this pain of love becomes intense to the Baüls for the Man of the mind, they go beyond any sense of distinction of caste. Perhaps this is why they are called '*Sahajiya*' (The simple followers). They easily unite with everyone in the society irrespective of caste and creed. They create an intense bond of unity with the universe.

—Santidev Ghosh : "Rabindranath O Banglar Baul" ("Rabindranath and the Baüls of Bengal"), *Rabindrasangeet Vichitra* (*Rabindrasangeet Miscellany*), Ananda Publishers Private Ltd., Calcutta, 1987, p. 97.

[Translated by me]

In his own folk songs, Tagore poignantly reveals this search for the Man of the mind. As he muses on :

Ami tarei khoonje vedai je ray mane amar mane.
Se aachhe vale
Amar aakash jude phote tara rate,
Prate phool Phoote ray vane amar vane
Se aachhe vale chokher tarar aaloy
Eta rooper khela ranger mela asim saadaay kaaloy.
Semor sange thaake vale
Amar ange ange haras jaagaay dakhin samirane.
Tari vani hathat uthe pure
Anmana kon taner majhe amar gaaner sure.

Dukher dole hathat more dolaay.
Kaazer majhe lukie theke amare kaaz bholaay
Semor chiradiner vale
Tari pulake mor palakguli bhare kshane kshane.

I seek Him alone who lives in my mind
As He does exist
Stars shine in the sky of my mind at night
Flowers bloom in my forest in the morning
As He does exist
In the light of the stars of the eyes
There's so much of play of beauty and feast of colour in endless black and white
As he remains with me.
The southern wind awakens joy in my every limb
His message it is that is filled
In the tune of my song amid an unmindful *taan*
He swings me in the sweep of sorrow all on a sudden
He conceals Himself amidst work and makes me forget my work
As eternal He is to me
It is His gladness that at times fills in my moments.

—Rabindranath Tagore : *Songs*, *Rabindra-Rachanavali*, Government of West Bengal, Calcutta, 1980. Vol. IV, No. 1097, p. 443.

[Translated by me]

The oneness of the Poet with the inner 'He' who lives within his mind and whose gladness fills him at every moment also opens out a new world of consciousness. He gets a new vision of seeing himself with the inward eyes of the All Seer. The folk world of the Baüls of Bengal have consciously or unconsciously taken a permanent position in his mind and the songs that reveal the philosophy of folk simplicity carry within themselves the simple vision of the Baüls. In one of his letters, Tagore elucidates his world of folk songs :

"Those who have read my writings know that I have expressed my devotion to *Baul Padavalis* in many of my writings. When I was at Shelaidah, I always met and talked with the group of Baüls. In many of my songs, I have accepted the tunes of the Baüls, and in many songs the union of the Baul tunes with the other tune-patterns with or without my knowledge. From this, it may be understood that the tunes and words of the Baüls have, at a certain period, easily mingled within me. I remember, in the very Shelaidah area, a Baul sang with an *ektara* (a single string musical instrument of the Baüls) :

Kothay pavo tare
Amar maner manush je re.

[Where shall I find Him,
The Man of my mind.]

The words are very simple, but their meaning brightened with a unique lustre in association with tuning. I heard from the non-scholar in his rustic tune and in simple language—the pain of not knowing Him least, whom one should know most, has been tuned in his voice "*Antaratara Yadayamatma* ("This soul is more endearing"). When I heard this message of the Upanishad from their voice as "Maner Manush" ("Man of the Mind"), I was greatly astonished. I have heard such a Baül's song as is incomparable in respect of simplicity of language, intensity of ideas and in empathy of tune. Just as it is in unison with the theories of knowledge, so is the composition of poetry coupled with the poignance of *Bhakti* (devotion). I do not believe there is any such brilliance anywhere as available in folk literature."

—Santidev Ghosh : "*Rabindranath O Banglar Baul*" ("Rabindranath and the Bauls of Bengal"), *Rabindrasangeet Vichitra* (*Rabindrasangeet Miscellany*), Ananda Publishers Private Limited, Calcutta, 1987, p. 98.

[Translated by me.]

For a basic concept of the folk songs of the *Vairagis* and the Bauls, Tagore came in close association with many of these homeless wanderers. He was deeply influenced by their deep study of life in its essence particularly their simple but pregnant explanations on life, death, immortality, peace, sorrows and sufferings, affiuence and emptiness. In one of his lectures delivered in 1910 in connection with the Bauls on the occasion of *Brahmatsov* he narrates :

> I few days ago I met two Bauls of a special community in the village. "Would you tell me about the speciality of your religion ?" Said I to them. One said, "Difficult to say, can't be said aright." The other said, "Of course, it can be said. It's easy. We say this : you'll have to know yourself at the very outset in accordance with the advice of the *Guru* (the Master). When I know myself, I find Him within that myself." I said, "Why don't you make all people of the world hear the words of your religion ?" "One who will be thirsty", he said, "would himself come to the Ganges." "Are you seeing that?" said I. "Is anyone coming?' With a very peaceful smile, the man said, "Everyone will come. Everyone will have to come."
>
> —*Ibid.*, pp. 98-99.
> [Translated by me]

The yearning of the Poet for unison with the ordinary people of everyday life to meet the Great Resident of his mind and the great intention within him to respond to the beckonings of the All Beautiful through the grass, leaves and birds of the forest unveil the world of light wherein he sees Him playing in the playhouse of his mind. Let's have a try to enter into the world of one of his folk songs :

Oder sathe melao jara charay tomar dhenu,
Tomar name vajaay jara venu.
Pasan diye vandha ghate ei-je kolahaler hate
Kena ami kiser lobhe enu.
Ki daak dake vaner pataguli, kaar isara-triner anguly !
Pranesh amar lilabhare khelen praner khelaghare,
Pakhir mukhe ei-je khavar penu.

Unite me with them who tend your cows,
Who play on the flute in your name,

On the stone-built bank, in this melee of chaos,
  Why and for what attraction did I come.
What's the call of the forest leaves, whose beckonings are
  thro' the grass
The God of my heart does play in the playhouse of the
  heart with all mysteries,
  This is the news that from the mouth of birds
  did I receive.

—Rabindranath Tagore : *Songs*, *Rabindra-Rachanavali*, Government of West Bengal, Calcutta, 1980, Vol. IV, No. 900, p. 373.

[Translated by me]

That the God of his heart is eternally playing in the playhouse of his mind, has been further intensified in the continual study of the mind made by the Poet. He seeks and seeks the mind frantically to listen to the sound of the flute played on by the unknown person. As he sings out :

Mon re ore mon, tumi kon sadhanar dhan.
Paine tomay paine, sudhu khunji saaraakshan.
Raater tara chokh na voje—andhakare tomay khonje,
Dike dike veday deke dakhin samiran.
Sagar jeman jagay dhwani, khonje nijer ratanmoni,
Temni kare aakaash chheye arun alo jaay je cheye—
Naam dhare tor vajaay vaanshi kon ajana jan.

Mind, O Mind, of what meditation you are the outcome
I find you not, only seeking all the time
The stars close not their eyes—seeking in darkness
  The southern wind calls on you everywhere
As the sea raises sound and seeks its own gem
  So the sunlight shines all over the sky
  Who is the unknown person that calls you by the name
  and plays on the flute.

—Rabindranath Tagore : *Songs*, *Rabindra Rachanavali*, Government of West Bengal, Calcutta, 1980, Vol. IV, No. 1613, p. 614.

[Translated by me]

The 'revelation of the Infinite in my own humanity', as the Poet feels within himself unfolds a new world of folk songs for him. It was an endless experience for him when he goes deep into the mystic world of the Bauls singing with a full-throated voice and delving deep into the endless mind. As he explains,

> 'The man of my Heart', to the Baul, is like a divine instrument perfectly tuned. He gives expression to infinite truth in the music of life. And the longing for the truth which is in us, which we have not yet realised, breaks out in the following Baul song :
>
> Where shall I meet him, the Man of my Heart ?
> He is lost to me and I seek him wandering from land to land,
>
> I am listless for that moonrise of beauty,
> Which is to light my life,
> Which I long to see in the fulness of vision, in gladness of heart.
>
> —Rabindranath Tagore : "An Indian Folk Religion", *Creative Unity*, Macmillan & Co. Ltd., London, 1962. pp. 78-79.

In his quest for the infinite mysteries of the mind, Tagore, like a self-seeking Baul, ponders over the unknown person who plays on the flute eternally to be a close associate of the mind. The tune of the flute is so intoxicating to him that it continually haunts him and the unending search is on.

Amare paday paday khepiye veday kon khyapa se !
Ore, akash jude mohan sure kee je vaje kon vatase
Gelo re gelo vela pagaler keman khela—
Deke se akul kare, dey na dhara.
Tare kanan giri khunje phiri, kende mari kon hutase.

Who is that intoxicator that goes on haunting me from one locality to the other
O, what lovely tuning is there all over the sky in the wind unknown

The day dies down what a game of the intoxicator
He spells a web in his call but remains away
I seek Him in forests and mountains, in what agony
do I go on crying.

—Rabindranath Tagore : *Songs, Rabindra Rachanavali*, Government of West Bengal, Calcutta, 1980, Vol. IV, No. 673, p. 292.

[Translated by me]

The insatiable spirit of simplicity as revealed in Tagore's folk songs brings forth a new image of the Poet as a man who is deeply involved in rural simplicity. He discovers a new world in the intoxicating beauty of the unending red road that runs through rural Bengal. He introspects on the infinity of his journey in a song that beats the pulse of rural life :

Gramchhada oi ranga matir path amar mon bhulay re.
Ore kar pane mon hat badiye lutie jaay dhulay re.
O je amay gharer vahir kare, paye-paye paye dhare—
O je kede amay niye jaay re jaay re kon chulaay re.
O je kon vake kee dhan dekhave, kon khane kee daay thekave—
Kothay giye sesh mele je bhevei na kulay re.

The red earthen path that leads beyond the village enchants my mind.
O, towards whom does the mind stretch out his hand and crumble into dust !
He drives me out of the room and clasps my feet
He snatches me away and goes where I know not
In which turn what wealth will he show and where and what would he involve responsibilities
Where the end will be met, I fail to reach the thought's end.

—Rabindranath Tagore : *Songs, Rabindra-Rachanavali*, Government of West Bengal, Calcutta, 1980, Vol. IV, No. 678, p. 293.

[Translated by me]

In the search for the Eternally Beautiful, the Poet, like a Baul, loves to be ever inquisitive. He does not find Him in abstraction but in purity of simple and serene dedication. As the Man of the heart lives in every heart, the Poet goes out to find Him anywhere and everywhere. The beauty in every aspect of Nature unfolds for him mysteries in abundance. The words unheard and the songs unsung are all treasured in the Poet's heart—whose wanderings and experiences within reveal His grace in poignance and lustre :

Amar praner manush aachhe praane,
Tai heri taay sakal khane.
Achhe se Nayantaray aalok-dharay, tai na haray—
Tai dekhi tay jethay sethay
Takai ami je dik-pane
Ami taar mukher katha sunvo vale gelaam kotha
Sona halo na, sona halo na—
Aaz phire ese nizer deshe ei-je suni
Suni tahar vani aapan gaane
Ke tora khoonjis tare kangal vese dware-dware
Dekha mele na, mele na—
O tora aay re dheye, dekh re cheye amar vooke—
Ore dekh re amar dui nayaane.

My man of my heart is in the heart
So I behold Him everywhere
In tqe stars of eyes, in the stream of light
He exists and so He is not lost
Ye, so I see Him anywhere and everywhere
Wherever I feast my eyes,
To hear Him speak I know not where I went
Alas, I heard Him not
Today in my own heart after my return
I hear His message in songs of mine
Who you are that seek Him like a beggar from
door to door

Never, never will you be able to meet Him.
O come in a hurry and see in my own breast,
In the two eyes of mine.

—Rabindranath Tagore : *Songs, Rabindra-Rachanavali*, Government of West Bengal, Calcutta, 1980, Vol. IV, No. 778, p. 329.

[Translated by me]

That the All Beautiful lives in his own heart, makes the Poet aware in all serenity. He has found out his own limitations—his so long neglect for the look within, his failure to feel the presence of the All Loving who remains in his joy and sorrow, play and happiness beside him. Like an ever smiling Baul, he sings out :

Amar hiar majhe lukiechhile dekhte ami pai ni.
Vahir pane chokh melechhi, hriday-panei chaai ni.
Amar sakal bhalovasay sakal aaghat sakal aashay
Tumi chhile amar kaachhe, tomar kaachhe jaai ni.
Tumi more ananda haye chhile amar khelay—
Anande tai bhulechhilem, ketechhe din helay.
Gopan rahi gabhir prane amar dukkha sukher gaane
Sur diyechha tumi, ami tomar gaan to gaani ni.

You remained hidden in my heart, I could not see
I looked wide outside, towards my heart I looked not,
In all my love, in all strokes and hopes
You were beside me, I went not nearby you
Like my joy you remained in my play
So I lost myself in joy, the days idly spent
In the poignant heart in secret, in my songs of joy and sorrow
You have given tunes but I did not sing your songs.

—Rabindranath Tagore : *Songs, Rabindra-Rachanavali*, Government of West Bengal, Calcutta, 1980, Vol, IV. No. 905, p. 375.

[Translated by me]

The agony of the Poet's failure to sing the song in unison with the tune of the All Beautiful also finds an humble confession as follows :

Amar Vela je jaay saanjh-velate
Tomar sure sure sur melate.
Amar ektaratir ekti tare gaaner vedan vaite naare,
Tomar sathe vare vare haar menechhi ei khelate,
Tomar sure sure sur melate
Amar e taar vandha kaachher sure
Oi vaansi je vaaje dure.
Gaaner lilar sei kinare jog dite ki savaai paare,
Visvahriday paravare raagraaginir jaal phelate—
Tomar sure sure sur melate.

My day ends in the evening
To be attuned with your tune
In the single string of my *ektara* the pain of my song cannot be carried over,
I have embraced defeat time and again in this play with you,
To be attuned with your tune.
This string of mine is meant for the tune nearby
Yonder is the flute that plays on in the distance
In that horizon of the mystery of song, can everyone take part
In the sea of the world of heart, can everyone cast his net
To be attuned with your tune !

—Rabindranath Tagore : *Songs*, *Rabindra-Rachanavali*, Government of West Bengal, Calcutta, 1980, Vol. IV, No. 1103, p. 445

[Translated by me]

Deeply influenced by the folk songs of the Bauls of Bengal Tagore wonders how the Baul singing for alms from door to door makes such a passionate revelation of love through his one-string instrument and long robe of patched-up rags on his back :

I stop and sit here on the road. Do not ask me to walk farther
If your love can be complete without mine, let me turn back from seeing you.
I have been travelling to seek you, my friend, for long;

Yet I refused to beg a sight of you, if you do not feel
my need
I am blind with market dust and midday glare,
and so wait my heart's lover in hopes that your own
love will send to find me out.

—Rabindranath Tagore : "An Indian Folk Religion", *Creative Unity*, Macmillan and Company Limited, London, 1962, p. 82.

Like a true lover as the Baul is, Tagore is in all ears to hear the words of the beloved who dwells in his heart. The words that are woven in the muse are crystallized in poignance of perfection and deeper sense of love :

Ami kaan pete roi amar aapan hridaygahan-dware
Kon gopanvaasir kaannahasir gopan katha sunivare—
Bhramar sethay hay vivagi nibhrita neel padma laagi re,
Kon raater paakhi gaay ekaki sangivihin andhakare.
Ke se mor kei va jaane, kichhu taar dekhi abha
Kichhu paai anumane, kichhu taar vujhi na va.
Majhe majhe taar vaarata amar bhasay paay ki katha re
O se amay jani paathay vani gaaner tane lukie taare.

I am in all ears at my own dense door of my heart
To hear the secret talks of the sorrows and smiles
of the hidden resident
The bees become stoical there to have the lone
blue lotus
The bird at night sings alone in darkness *sans* companion
Who she is none knows, behold I some of her lustres
Some I have in assumption, some I do not make out.
Oft her message what a word does receive in my language!
O, I know she sends message in the tune of songs concealed
in strings.

—Rabindranath Tagore : *Songs, Rabindra-Rachanavali*, Government of West Bengal, Calcutta, 1980, Vol. IV, No. 1197, p. 475.

[Translated by me]

The golden touch of love that the Poet has received by means of inward devotion to the All Beautiful has made the heart wide open to embrace Him in all adoration. A total unison of his all sacrificing self and the Divine self of the All Beautiful brings forth the song of dedication in poised simplicity. The moment of the great awakening blooms in music :

Ami tarei jani tarei jani amay je jan apan jane—
Tari dane davi amar jaar adhikar amar dane.
Je amare chinte pare se chenatei chini tare—
Eki alo chenar pathe tar prane aar amar prane.
Apan maner andhakare dhaklo jara
Ami tader madhye apanhara.
Chhuinye dilo sonar kathi, ghumer dhaka gelo phati—
Nayan amar chhutechhe tar alo-kara mukher pane.

I know Him, I do know Him who endears me as His very own
I do demand His gift, and He has His right in mine.
I know Him just as how He knows me
The same light of recognition shines the hearts His and mine,
Those who covered them in the darkness of their heart
I lose myself among them.
He touched the golden wand and tore apart the covering of slumber
My eyes are running towards His beaming face of light.

—Rabindranath Tagore : *Songs*, *Rabindra-Rachanavali*, Government of West Bengal, Calcutta, 1980, Vol. IV, No. 1627, p. 619.

[Translated by me]

One recalls Tagore's own inspiration received from the folk-singers of Bengal, specially Jnāndās whose devout expression finds serene impression upon the above. Perhaps the following folk song of Jnāndās translated by Tagore himself, has a deeper appeal to his own folk song :

I had travelled all day and was tired; then I bowed my head.

towards thy kingly court still far away
The night deepened, a longing burned in my heart.
Whatever the words I sang, pain cried through them—
for even my songs thirsted—
O my Lover, my Beloved, my Best in all the world.

When time seemed lost in darkness thy hand dropped its sceptre to take up the lute and strike the uttermost chords :
And my heart sang out.
O my Lover, my Beloved, my Best in all the world.

Ah, who is this whose arms enfold me ?
Whatever I have to leave, let me leave; and whatever I have to bear, let me bear.
Only let me walk with thee,
O my Lover, my Beloved my Best in all the world.

Descend at whiles from thy high audience hall, come down amid joys and sorrows
Hide in all forms and delights, in love,
And in my heart sing thy songs,—
O my Lover, my Beloved, my Best in all the world.

—Rabindranath Tagore : "An Indian Folk Religion", *Creative Unity*, Macmillan & Co. Ltd., London, 1962, pp. 89-90.

For an eternal seeker of joy as Tagore is, the 'Best in all the world' cannot remain dissociated from him for long. The playtime is almost over but the Poet, blind as he considers himself, seeks the light from the Great Illuminator to dispel all darkness. The throbbing moments have come, The pains of his heart have presented him with the blessings of the Best. He now feels that the strings of his lyre—the lyre of the heart—are tightened anew. The conflict between the good and the evil in him is no more. And now the fulness born of the blessings of the Best is bloomed in muse :

Ami jakhan chilem andha
Surer khelay vela gechhe pai ni to ananda

Khelagharer deyal genthe kheyal nie chhilem mete
Bhit bhenge jei ele ghare ghuchlo amar vandha
Sukher khela aar rochena, peyechhi ananda.
Bhisan amar, rudra amar, nidra gelo kshudra amar—
Ugra vyathay nutan kare vandhle amar chhanda.
Je din tumi agniveshe sav-kichhu more nile eshe
Se din ami purna halem ghuchlo amar dvandva
Dukkhasukher pare tomay peyechhi ananda.

When I was bereft of vision
My time was spent in the play of tunes but I found no joy.
Building the walls of the playhouse, I was rapt in whims
When you came by cracking the foundation, my bondage is over
The game of happiness I like no more, I have found joy.
O my Terrible, my Fierce, my little slumber is gone
You've tuned up my rhythm with violent pains anew
The day when in the guise of fire you took away my all
I became perfect on that day and my conflicts came to an end.
O joy, I have been in unison with you beyond the banks of sorrow and happiness.

—Rabindranath Tagore : *Songs*, *Rabindra-Rachanavali*, Government of West Bengal, Calcutta, 1980. Vol. IV, No. 1614, p. 615.

[Translated by me]

Like a stoic Baul singer, the Poet feels within himself the eternal source of joy that shows him to be a traveller of freedom and spontaneity. As he sings out :

Kee dhwani vaaje
Gahanachetanamaajhe.
Kee anande uchchhvasila
Mama tanuveena gahanachetanamaajhe
Manapranahara sudha-jhara
Parashe bhavana udasina.

What a sound echoes
Amid consciousness deep and serene !
With what a joy
Did the *Veena* on my arm splash
On the consciousness deep and serene.
Stealing the mind and the heart and pouring pleasant juice
And with its touch the thoughts stoical.

—Rabindranath Tagore : *Songs, Rabindra-Rachanavali,* Government of West Bengal, Calcutta, 1980, Vol. IV, No. 1612, p. 614.

[Translated by me]

As an ardent devotee of the All Beautiful to whom the Poet has, like a Baul completely surrendered himself, he wants to find solace in the presence of the Omnipresent. Let the heart of the Poet be seized by Him. Let it be the abode of the All Beautiful. The search of the Poet for the Man of the heart has almost come to an end. The heart is yet to be free from the stains of darkness and ignorance, emptiness and desolation. Let the Most Beloved come to the breast of the Poet and speak the words of eternal message and destroy all inconsistencies and imperfections from which the Poet yet suffer. Here is the song of humble submission :

Tumi evar amay laho he nath, laho
Evar tumi phiro na he—
Hriday kede niye raho.
Je din gechhe toma vina tare aar phire chahina,
Jaak se dhulate.
Ekhan tomar aaloy jeevan mele jena jagi aharaha.
Kee aaveshe Keeser kathay phirechhi he jathay tathay
Pathe Prantare.
Evar vooker kaachhe O mukh rekhe tomar aapan vanni kaho
Kata kalush kata phanki ekhono je achhe vaaki
Maner gopane
Amay taar laagi aar phirayona—
Taare aagun diye daho.

Please accept me now, O my Lord, accept me.
O, Please do not refuse me now,

Remain seizing my heart.
I do not want again the day lost *sans* you
Let it go to dust
Now let me allow to remain awake day and night
By expanding my life in your light
With what an aroma and in what a word
Have I roamed everywhere
In cities and in fields !
Tell me now the message of your own
Hiding your face nearer my heart.
So many stains and so many truancies
Are yet remained in the depth of the mind
Please do not tell me to go back once more for these,
Burn these with fire.

—Rabindranath Tagore : *Songs*, *Rabindra-Rachanavali*, Government of West Bengal, Calcutta, 1980, Vol. IV, No. 733, p. 312.

[Translated by me]

Elsewhere, the same sense of humble submission for discipline of the soul has been expressed by the Poet :

Life of my life, I shall ever try to keep my body pure, knowing that thy living touch is upon all my limbs.

I shall ever try to keep all untruths out from my thoughts, knowing that thou art that truth which has kindled the light of reason in my mind.

I shall ever try to drive all evils away from my heart and keep my love in flower, knowing that thou hast thy seat in the inmost shrine of my heart.

And it shall be my endeavour to reveal thee in my actions, knowing it is thy power gives me strength to act.

—Rabindranath Tagore : *Song Offerings* (*Geetanjali*), Macmillan Pocket Tagore Edition, Macmillan India Limited, New Delhi, 1983, No. IV, p. 3.

Perhaps Tagore was greatly influenced by the Baul's prayer to the All Beautiful who submits himself to the will of Him by singing :

I am the boat, you are the sea, and also the boatman.
Though you never make the shore, though you let me sink,
Why should I be foolish and afraid ?
Is the reaching the shore a greater prize than losing myself
With you ?
If you are only the haven, as they say, then what is the sea ?
Let it surge and toss me on its waves, I shall be content.
I live in you, whatever and however you appear.
Save me or kill me as you wish, only never leave me in others' hands.

—Rabindranath Tagore : "An Indian Folk Religion", *Creative Unity*, Macmillan & Co. Ltd., London, 1962, p. 88.

The feeling of 'living within' the All Beautiful as the folk singers like the Baüls of Bengal earnestly crave for, also inspires Tagore to be in all communion with Him. Let the Man of the heart, as he thinks, come in the inmost core of the heart. In darkness or in pangs of separation He is there awaiting the beckoning of the heart and so the Poet sings like a self-winning Baul :

Se je maner manush, kena taare vasiye rakhis nayanadware.
Daak-na re tor vooker bhitar, nayan bhaasuk nayana-dhaare.
Jakhan nibhve aalo, aasve raati, hridaye dish aasan paati—
Aasve se je sangopane Vichchhederi andhakaare.
Taar aasaa jaaoaar gopan pathe
Se aasve jaave aapan mate
Taare vaandhve vale jei karo pan se thakena thake vaandhan—
Sei vaandhane mane mane vaandish keval aapanaare.

The Man of the heart He is, why do you keep Him seated beside the door of your eyes;

Why not call Him in your breast, let eyes be washed away
with the streams of eyes!
When lights will be extinguished and the night will come,
spread the seat in your heart
In darkness of separation will He in secret arrive
In His secret path of arrival and departure
In His own accord will He come and depart
When you promise to bind Him, He remains not,
the string does remain
Bind yourself aside with that string alone.

—Rabindranath Tagore : *Songs, Rabindra-Rachanavali,* Government of West Bengal, Calcutta, 1980, Vol. IV, No. 1392, p. 538.

[Translated by me]

Like a true visionary, Tagore involves himself completely with the inner world of communion with the All Beautiful. As he sings, he always feels His presence and as he roams in his own world like a homeless wanderer he sees the Omnipresent in all brilliance. The traveller's song on the way makes him aware of the passing moments of life. Like the folk-artist who prays for meeting the All Beautiful singing : O Guru, my days are over, the evening has come, please oar me to You, he also awaits His green signal for communion amid the fragrance of unknown flowers. Only His love that knows no distinction acts as the guiding force within him from time to time :

Kaandale tumi more bhalovasari ghaaye—
Nivid vedanate pulak laage gaaye.
Tomar abhisaare javo agama-paare
Chalite pathe-pathe vaajuk vyatha paaye.
Paraane vaaje vaanshi, nayane vahe dhaara—
Dukher Maadhurite karila dishahaara.
Sakali nive kede. dive na tavu chhede—
Mon sare na jete, phelile e kee daaye.

Thou hast made me weep with the stroke of thy love,
In intense pain I feel joy in me

I shall go to the shores of the unreachable in
search of thee
Let pain tune on during my journey on every avenue
The flute plays on in the heart, streams roll on thro' eyes
The beauty of sorrow made me lose direction
Thou would snatch away all, yet would Thou leave
nothing
The mind does not desire to depart, O in what a mess
hast Thou bound me !

—Rabindranath Tagore : *Songs, Rabindra-Rachanavali*, Government of West Bengal, Calcutta, 1980, Vol. IV, No. 1554, p. 595.

[Translated by me]

The world of Tagore's folk songs is, indeed, the world of beauty in poignance. It is a world that invites all to surrender themselves to the will of God whom he adores as All Beautiful. It is the world that beckons love and sorrow, pain and pleasure side by side and, of course, simultaneously. It is a world that spells out Beauty from ignorance and hatred, and from falsehood and hypocrisy. It is a world that marvels in purity of mind and heart. For the Poet, the journey of the singer is all the way exciting. The evergreen lustre, the myriad beauty of birds, beasts, flowers, streams, forests and hills side by side with the happy reminiscence of the loving sweet days of yore or those tinged with sorrow or desolation—all present him to prepare himself for a serene and blessed prayer to the All Beautiful by tuning on the string of his *ektara* :

Jani tomar preme sakal premer vaani meshe,
Ami seikhaanetei mukti khunji diner seshe.
Sethay premer charam saadhan, jaay khase taar sakal
vandhan—
Mor hriday-paakhir gagan tomar hridaydeshe.
Ogo, jani aamar sranta diner sakal dhaara
Tomar gabhir raater santimajhe klantihaara,
Amar dehe dharar paras tomar sudhay halo saras—
Amar dhulari dhan tomar majhe nutan veshe.

I know in thy love the message of all love mingles
I seek my salvation in it alone at the day's end.
The greatest meditation of love is there, all its bonds are loosened
In thy heart is the sky of the bird of my heart
O Dear, know I that all the streams of my tired days
Become tireless in the bliss of thy dense-deep night
The touch of the earth in my body has become lively with thy drink
The very wealth of my dust adores within Thee in a new pattern.

—*Ibid.*, No. 1528, p. 585.

[Translated by me]

For a folk-singer like Tagore, the only way to be in perfect unison with All Beautiful is to become a Sufi and follow *Muraqaba.*

Who else than Rabindranath Tagore sings more gracefully in contemplation of the nearness of the Divine—the *maner manush* or the Man of the heart—as the Sufis do ?

FULNESS IN EDUCATION AND SOCIAL CHANGE : TAGOREAN VIEWPOINTS

Education is always a look within, an endless journey, an askance eternal. It paves for new dimensions and awakens new sensibilities in mankind. It continually signals an individual to go ahead with newer visions of humanity. It calls forth for the fruits of the best of everyone to be an excellent exponent of the society.

To be an excellent exponent of the society in the real sense of the term, one necessitates something more than mere excellence. This something more beckons social harmony leading to global cohesion. For a change in the society in which an individual lives, this sense of cohesion indicates a very significant departure. It is this significant departure that endears the great social goal of humanity—*Vasudhaiva Kutumvakam.* Live and let others live in harmony under the same umbrella of the One Big Family of Mankind.

How can an individual be inspired to live so ? How can he be a true social member amid the global society of harmony ? How can he do away with the petty desires and inclinations of his little self, the little 'I', and justify himself to be worthy of the wider self, the greater 'I', so that he might prove himself truly social ? All these and a host of other questions await an appropriate response through education and education for fulness alone. Rabindranath's own social philosophy of education points to this assertion. An individual, as he rightly remarks, is totally meaningless unless he is of any use to the society. He becomes a cipher in the great company of cohesion. He turns himself into a social lunatic in the senseless asylum of individuality. The history of human civilization is replete with such asylums stuffed with lunatic individuals dreaming marvels in massacres. Destruction, the so-called happy outcome of heretic individuality, shows its back towards social education and, for that end in view, social progress.

Rabindranath was always aware of this massacre of individuality baked in the fire of individual whims and caprices and fabricated in sham pomp and grandeur. The masses remain masses of this senseless game of individual greed and gaiety and the social strata of life as encountered and negotiated through this showmanship and mockeries of individuality suffers from a cancerous growth of obsession and passivity. Tagore's call for the revival of social norms for goodness, truth and beauty through awakening of individual sensibilities marks an altogether newer avenue of social awareness. It is awareness born not out of affluence nor even of passion but out of conscience and of contemplation. The lost man in the society is yearning for the beckoning of consciousness nursed in a harmonized society to prove the fact that he is never lost. Hence fulness in education for fulness of the society.

Tagore has nothing unusual to contribute as a social reformer. Rather are his very words of social awareness synchronized in patterns of desirable human behaviour. He never sermonizes nor does he ever pose to be sermonized through affluence of words that could have made fireworks in theories of social transformation normally appreciated as a symbol of expertized opinion, but, in actuality, end in futility. He believes in sincerity both in action and in contemplation as an unparalleled social thinker.

Everyone is aware of the fact that, like a true visionary. Tagore wanted to infuse the spirit of cultural synthesis for better social change. This synthesis, as he thinks, makes a better homeland for every mind to be more potent in thought and action instead of mere toying with utopian ideologies and contemplation. In fact, the very thought of challenging the shortcomings of the western culture and civilization at the crucial stage of crisis during the Second World War and at the fag end of his life proves the fact that he was always a foreseer of the synthesis of culture and society.

While making an analysis of the true spirit of the history of India from the standpoint of social and cultural synthesis, Rabindranath goes deep into the problems of cultural incoherence and suggests a newer approach to rebuild the foundations of the society with renovated ideas of the role of history. In his essay on "Chhātrasāsantantra", later translated into English as "Indian Students and Western Teachers" and published in *The Modern Review*, April 1916, he remarks :

> The history of man takes different shapes in different countries. The history of India has also its specialities. From the very beginning of her history, we have been visualizing that this country is not meant for a particular nation or a particular civilization. Just as the Aryan civilization is true in this country, so is the Dravidian civilization. In this country, the Muslims are not less big than the Hindus. For this very reason, the very history of this country has, like an enormous meteor, become blurred with the vapour of clashes of diverse conflicts. We have been encountering the commotion of different forces in this history but we have not yet visualized the outcome of an undivided historical image. The distinct cry of an eternally inseparable "I" out of this expanded vastness has not yet awakened.
>
> —Rabindranath Tagore : '*Chhatrasasantra*', *Siksha*, Visva-Bharati, 1973, p. 165.
>
> [Translated by me]

Like a great social synthesizer, Tagore makes an ardent appeal to the finer sensibilities of mankind—the sensibilities of the heart—to bring about a certain form of social cohesion in the spurt of emotion. Accordingly, he does not want that our pupils should have a factional knowledge and experience of the history of the world—a history that is alienated from the main socio-cultural stream of people living far or near. Like a social revolutionary, he first made our countrymen conscious of the fact that even the history of the British—their social and cultural manners, customs and traditions in their best possible patterns—greatly demand emulation and appreciation. As he categorically states :

> ...I am observing that as there are the Aryans, the Dravidians, as the Muslims so are also the British. The real history of India is, therefore, not only our history but also the history of the British. Now we will have to see if these different parts of history are properly synchronized and the whole thing becomes a part of the living body. We have no ability to eliminate any of the parts. We could not leave the Muslims aside nor would we be able to leave the English. This is not due to the absence of physical strength, the very nature of the history is this. It is not the history of a particular nation but it is the chemical process of the history of humanity.
>
> —Rabindranath Tagore : "*Chhatrasasantra*", *Siksha*, Visva-Bharati, 1973. p. 165.
>
> [Translated by me]

To eliminate the rest of the social systems of the world from the history of one's own country is to be deprived of the great elements of humanity. Tagore warned far ahead of today's modern thinkers and social scientists that the art of living in association with the global society is the first lesson of humanity. It is also the lesson that enables everyone to be equipped with the weapons of social consciousness to fight against any communal violence and any other social disruptive forces. The education of today hardly takes any major role to negotiate the undesirable tensions of the modern society. It is interesting to note in this connection that Rabindranath visualized these sad consequences of the so-called modern civilization in his unique introspective pattern of thoughts and wanted to revitalize the universal spirit of Brotherhood of Mankind, which finally took shape in his idea of the foundation of Visva-Bharati. It is, indeed, the idea of fulness in education through which a transvaluation of social norms and values can be significantly brought out. With this definite idea in view Tagore shows in his educational thoughts and experiments at Visva-Bharati that not from the ivory tower of alienation but from the platform of common social day to day pattern of life all social inconsistencies need a change—a thrilling and pulsating change, of course.

In his own Visva-Bharati whose motto is, as he firmly declares *Yatra Visam bhavatyekanidam*—an unparalleled excerpt from the Upanisad—where the world makes its home in a single nest, the social evolution of mankind has been considered from the grassroot levels of human consciousness. And whatever educational principles and procedures, methods and strategies are innovated and practised in performances are all in the pipeline of the total social welfare of humanity.

From a study of Tagore's own concept of the role of the university for social change as revealed in "*Visva-Vidyālayer Rūp*", an address delivered by him to the students and the teachers of the University of Calcutta in December, 1932 which was later published in the form of a booklet in 1933, one might have a multidimensional approach to human advancement and civilization. As he observes.

> There is no need for elaborate description on the origin of the university. What I want to say in general is : To protect and disseminate the special love, glory and responsibility felt by a particular country, a particular nation on the discipline naturally refers to the first creation of a universiy. The intention that is at the grassroot level of all creation is the outcome of that very will-force of the country. At the root of this intention lies the grandeur of power. That grandeur wants to express itself in continual spontaneity by grace; it cannot be dissuaded.
>
> All civilized countries make the hospitality of erudition wide open for their own universities. One who has excess of wealth welcomes the guests. The host admits the universe in his own guest house. At Nalanda, India opened the institution for dissemination of her own knowledge for all the invitees of her own country and abroad. On that day she felt that she has so wealth in abundant quantities as to find her highest success in contributing to mankind. In most of the countries of the western continent this guest-house of learning is existent. There is no difference between the native and the foreigner there. In the universal sphere of learning there, every man is reciprocally very own. In almost all parts of the society the barriers of dissociation

are becoming unsurmountable everyday. Only in this great pilgrimage of knowledge the invitation for mankind persisted. This is because to admit poverty and austerity in this sphere is the most alleviating factor of the self for a civilized race. The courtyard of the fortunate country is wide open towards the universe in this sphere.

—Rabindranath Tagore : "*Visvavidyālayer Rūp*" *Siksha*, Visva-Bharati, 1973, pp. 207-208.

[Translated by me]

For a perfect social change, education cannot but cater to the needs of the society and, for that end in view, universities, colleges, schools and all other forms of educational institutions must uphold the highest aim of education : 'to follow', as Tennyson's Ulysses untiringly strives, 'knowledge like a sinking star'. When education makes avenues for human development the social upbringing of every one is directed towards this pursuit of knowledge. Added to this social upbringing, Rabindranath goes ahead with one more intrinsic and vital factor of human development and human civilization. It is social refinement that marks the glory of fulness in education. It is also a characteristic feature of social advancement. It enables every social being to come out of his little self, the little 'I', and to dedicate himself whole-heartedly towards the cause of the greater self. the greater "I", for through continual refinement within himself he understands the truth of the great Upanishadic saying : *bhumaiva sukham nālpe sukhamasti*,—happiness lies not in littleness but in vastness.

The arduous and ardent task of the university, as Rabindranath thinks, is to prepare an attitude towards this greater goodness of a greater society to usher forth with endless avenues of erudition and excellence. Not by imitation but through exercise and excellence of one's own individuality can one contribute most effectively towards social fulfilment. Then, and then only, a seat of learning becomes a universal temple of altruism, a church for cherished ideals of social oneness, a mosque for magnificence of personality or a synagogue of serenity of passions and meditations.

While analysing the role of education for greater individual and social consciousness, Rabindranath delineates the ancient history of the Indian seats of learning and elucidates the function of universities for the emancipation of all round goodness. As he observes :

> There is an aspect of knowledge, which is subjective. It is existent in the greed for collection of materials for knowledge. It excites the pomp of scholarship. No great inspiration finds enthusiasm towards this storehouse of the spendthrift. The reference to the era of the great Indian universities that I had made had meditation within it. This is because it had not the aim to fill in the storehouse. Its objective was to enkindle the universal mind, awakening and creation of character. The ideal of total humanity as reflected in the mind of India in knowledge, action and in ideas of the heart was to be infused through this endeavour in the lives of all for eternity towards economic and other worldly abilities and not towards the intellect alone.
>
> This is also applicable to the institutions of Nalanda and Vikramsila. In that era, the people of the country intensively understood the invaluable price of learning. There is no doubt that encompassing it in total fulness, the desire to establish universal seat of knowledge naturally came in the Indian mind.
>
> —Rabindranath Tagore : "*Visvavidyālayer Rup*", *Siksha*, Visva-Bharati, 1973, p. 202.
>
> [Translated by me]

That the social awakening of the masses need an enlightened seat of advancement of learning can hardly be ignored. Tagore wants every educational institution to play this vital role of bringing about social consciousness so that the union between thought and action, experimentation and contemplation pave worthier avenues of emancipation of individuality. Education turned into reverence for what is just, pure, serene and simple changes the whole gamut of the socially distressed people's thoughts and activities and plays a vital role in orienting people's behavioural bankruptcies. Tagore, therefore, emphasizes on re-thinking on character-crisis which is at the root of crisis of civilization. Social bruises affect humanity most and the only way to negotiate these social maladies is, as he rightly thinks and acts accordingly, to utilize the endless strength inherent in education. Obviously, he has to choose an avenue ostracised by education-shy political thinkers whose ideas and policies of social re-construction are primarily inclined not towards spread of education for fulness of man but mere country's independence paying a heavy price in utter confusion and chaos in social stratas of life as a consequence.

Not mere utilitarianism but fulness in education can alone bring about desirable social change. As a matter of fact, Rabindranath comes nearer to Mahatma Gandhi who also wants to bring about social change through mass awakening of consciousness in his theories and experimentations on *Sarvodaya* which is the education for all round sympathy and cohesion. A muse misunderstood and more often than not unheard, *Sarvodaya* is the lesson of moral and ethical purity of perfection that contributes a lot to the welfare of the global society.

Admittedly, the ideal of universal goodness of the society that Gandhi holds up in his prayer speech comes nearer to that of Tagore's education for sympathy and universal brotherhood of mankind. As a champion of the eternal soul of mankind, Gandhi highlights global awakening through emergence of the spirit of self-sacrifice :

> A truly independent and free India would rush to the help of her neighbours in distress. A man whose spirit of sacrifice does not go beyond his own community, himself becomes, and makes his community, selfish. The logical sequel of self-sacrifice is that the individual sacrifices himself for the community, the community for the district, the district for the province, the province for the nation, and the nation for the world. A drop from the ocean perishes without doing any good. As a part of the ocean, it shares the glory of carrying on its bosom whole fleets of mighty ships.
>
> —M.K. Gandhi : Prayer Speech, February 26, 1947, Pyarelal : *Mahatma Gandhi—The Last Phase*, Navajivan Publishing House, Ahmedabad, Vol. I, Book 2, p. 189.

Elsewhere, while explaining the true spirit of non-violence, *Satyagraha* as he solemnly says, Gandhi elucidates the role of non-violence from the standpoint of unconditional and spontaneous outcome of the spirit of social responsibilities on the part of every human being to manifest the fulness of his moral and social development. A true social revolutionary, Gandhian education for social competency is, like Tagore, born of the sense of social consciousness and self-sacrifice :

> The action of *Satyagraha* proceeds through the technique of identification and involvement. By suffering for truth and justice in his own person cheerfully instead of inflicting suffering upon the opponent, the *Satyagrahi* establishes his spiritual identity with the opponent and awakens in him the feeling that he cannot trust him (the *Satyagrahi*) without hurting his own personality.
>
> —Pyarelal : "Gandhiji's Satyagraha—Its Technique and Application", *Gandhian Outlook and Technique*, Ministry of Education, Government of India, 1953, p. 383.

For a society with all avenues of consciousness, Tagore wants dissemination of education from humane perspectives. He feels the urge for support from within by means of self-realization and self-activity and not from outside as Gandhi warns from time to time. Even economic self-sufficiency for social and economic synchronization as Tagore visualizes and acts accordingly is a precondition to the growth and development of national peace and prosperity. None can deny the fact that it is Tagore, and Tagore alone who wants to make room for scientific and technical expertise in the forms of practical operations in farms and fields, in laboratories and lands. The scientific use of machineries and appliances, the appropriate applications of medicines like pesticides and drugs for negotiating white ants, wilts, caterpillars and bacterial diseases of seedlings and plants have brought about dramatic and revolutionary changes in the sphere of agriculture in modern times. But who ignores that Tagore was the pioneer in this sphere of revolution because it was he who first launched such experiments in his own Institute for Rural Development at Sriniketan with all latest know-hows in science and technology ? Added to these, what is more astonishing and interesting is that in order to show his genuine concern for improvement in agriculture he sent his own son to the U.S.A. to undergo specialization in agriculture and engaged him on his return to look after cultivation and instil mass awareness in agricultural development thereby enhancing social advancement.

Elimination of social superstitions, apathy and ignorance is one of the fundamental aspects of fulness in education and Tagore's social thinking is primarily geared to this end in view. As he considers illiteracy a bondage and apathy a human curse, his entire thesis on fulness in education is based on freedom of the human mind.

While explaining the relation between aims and education in the context of human freedom, Tagore analyses the role of education for social transformation as follows :

> What I want to say is : in no country education cannot be completely imparted from the school and in our country, too, it is not being done. The power to digest is not attained from the shop of the sweet-sellers, only food is prepared there. Where human power is subject to endeavour to a large extent his learning is synchronized with his nature there only. Owing to the absence of proper direction of our life, we are failing to instil our bookish education in our heart.
>
> —Rabindranath Tagore : "*Lakshya O Siksha*" ("Aims and Education"), *Siksha*, Visva-Bharati, 1973, p. 133
>
> [Translated by me]

As a serene social visionary, Tagore makes an indepth analysis of the role of humanity from the standpoint of the soils of bondage that create favourable ground for social emancipation. As he deeply observes :

> In fact, the sphere of power is limited to any nation from some aspects or other. Everywhere the inherent nature and

> the external circumstances make a mutual harmony and determine their own sphere out of their own. This is because to diverge nature is not to utilize itself. In no country, favourable circumstances provide people with unbarred freedom because it ends in futility. What Providence provide us is proportionately given; in that case differences of division might be more or less existent.
>
> —Rabindranath Tagore : "*Lakshya O Siksha*", (Aims and Education"), *Siksha*, Visva-Bharati, 1973, pp. 133-34.
>
> [Translated by me]

From broader social perspectives, Tagore makes a more intensive approach to available resources for social and human fulfilment. The aesthetics of applicabilily is what is to be seriously taken into account. Therefore, the first important role of an individual as a social human being is to approach every aspect of social development from a wider perspective of vision where no policy is determined by fixed regulated principles of belief or superstition. The freedom of undertaking every kind of social activity signifies the freedom of human fulfilment. This opens out a new vista of creativity and inquisitiveness that determines the excellence of an individual as a social human being.

Tagore makes the point of exercise of freedom of activity in actualizing it for social welfare very clearly when he observes :

> It is not therefore, greater for man as to what he receives than how he will accept and utilize it. Whatever stands in the way of that power of acceptance or paralizes it under any social or mental circumstances, is the root of all massacres. Where mankind fails to allow anything to be accepted with enquiries and indicates to accept everything little or great with streamlined belief and regulated principles, however favourable the circumstances might be there, humanity cannot but be duped down. We pine for our narrowness of circumstances, but we do not at all know what actually our circumstances are. * * * As we can-

not bank upon the nature of mankind we are in a position to completely forget that unless man is allowed to commit errors he is not allowed to learn.

—*Ibid.*, p. 134.
[Translated by me]

An advocate of emancipation of mankind from all narrowness of outlook, Tagore further elucidates the role of freedom for fulness of individuality in a wider social perspective of vision :

There is no greater poverty than considering one's conditions superior to one's power.

—*Ibid.*, p. 134.
[Translated by me]

That the truth of humanity is the truth of emancipation of total human welfare points towards the fulness of education as a positive outcome of social change. And, admittedly, this truth of humanity is the inherent spirit of freedom exercised for individual as well as social welfare. Tagore visualizes this intrinsic force of freedom as the avenue of negotiating the crisis of modernity. As he observes :

What is of greatest value in case of human aspiration can never be unpursuable. And I do believe in this. If the freedom of our nation does not lie beside, it must lie above. We must not forget it even for a single moment. To expand all around by spreading branches and shoots is becoming our object of vision, and, for this, we have assumed it to be the only criterion for expansion. But the movement upward is also the movement of life. Therein also the fruits of success are brought forth in fulness. The main point is : whether this side or that, the attraction of vastness must be admitted. We will have to become great, and greater than what we are. We will have to give all ears to that message which pulls us out of the corners, which strengthens us to easily sacrifice ourselves, which does not enclose our aspiration in the cage between the walls of the office

> and the job. When this movement will be instilled in our national life, this force will become strong, then, at every moment we would begin to surmount our circumstances. Then no delicacies in our external conditions would slightly ashame us.
>
> —Rabindranath Tagore : "*Lakshya O Siksha*" ("Aims and Education"), *Siksha*, Visva-Bharati, 1973, p. 135.
>
> [Translated by me]

To transform the society in accordance with fulness of growth and development of human personality as visualized by Tagore in his thoughts on the freedom of every individual in our national life is long overdue. The history of human progress cannot but accept the truth that man must triumph over his own limitations under any trying circumstances.

Already, the society marooned in unrestricted consumption has created anomalies in individuals. A passive society, as Tagore clearly indicates, always shows its back towards the desirable spirit of social culture and civilization. Fromm has made a significant analysis of this consumption-hungry society of modern times, that comes nearer to Tagorean thoughts on social development and modernity :

> Man today is fascinated by the possibility of buying more, better, and especially, new things. He is consumption-hungry. The act of buying and consuming has become a compulsive, irrational aim because it is an end in itself, with little relation to the use of, or pleasure in the things bought and consumed. To buy the latest gadget, the latest model of anything that is on the market, is the dream of everybody, in comparison to which the real pleasure in use is quite secondary.
>
> —Erich Fromm : *The Sane Society*, Holt, Rinehart & Winston, Inc., New York, 1955, p. 135.

That education is becoming almost alien to the individual upbringing of every one in the society to be socially aware of others' advantages and inconveniences, is fast losing its ground.

Today's society bears no stamp of education in the true sense of the term. As Fromm further elucidates :

> Modern man, if he dared to be articulate about his concept of heaven, would describe a vision which would look like the biggest department store in the world, showing new things and gadgets, and himself having plenty of money with which to buy them. He would wander around open-mouthed in this heaven of gadgets and commodities, provided only that there were ever more and newer things to buy, and perhaps that his neighbours were just a little less privileged than he.
>
> —Erich Fromm : *Op. cit.* p. 135

The educative principle of co-operation that Tagore wanted to introduce in the country by means of dissemination of education for social awareness needs rethinking. The approach to villages in particular where life is yet more or less synchronized with the spirit of social sympathy necessitates reorientation so that education might contribute amply towards social fulness. As a great liberating force, education, as Tagore thinks, makes newer avenues of social emancipation.

To eradicate social complexities in order to bring about better social environment, education, as Tagore categorically asserts, is the only way to negotiate imbalances particularly the irritating intellectual ones. A positive social thinker for the common social goodness of every individual, he always endeavours to make a balanced rationale in intellectual inconsistencies that have at present been seriously looked into from the standpoint of human evolution by modern thinkers. As Simpson characteristically remarks :

> Some differences in degree of intelligence may be desirable, but the point is debatable and in any case the raising of the average nearer to the present maximum is evidently desirable. Such changes as these would require provision of optimum environmental conditions, but could not be achieved by this means alone; genetic selection in the existing variability of the species would also be required. There

is ample evidence that intelligence is if not strictly determined at least strictly limited as to potentialities by inheritance. Even temperament is apparently to some degree hereditary and correlated with physical structure, better knowledge of which would facilitate selection.

Such changes, involving differences in distribution of existing characters within the human population, are evolutionary but they are of limited scope. Ultimate progress beyond these limits would necessarily involve the development of new characters in the human organism. Probably the new character most surely necessary for evolution beyond the present limits is an increase in intelligence above the existing maximum. Human progress depends on knowledge and learning, and the capacity for these is conditioned by intelligence. Most scientists are already aware that the progress of science is being impeded by the fact that the most brilliant men simply do not have enough learning capacity to acquire all the details of more than increasingly narrow segments of the field of knowledge. Only a very stupid person can believe that mankind is already intelligent enough for its own good.

—George Gaylord Simpson : *The Meaning of Evolution*, Mentor Books, New York, 1951, pp. 170-71.

For a true evolution of human society and, for that end in view, humanity, Tagore accelerates a rational, humane and unsnobbish approach to human creativity that has its roots in social excellences. He does not believe in mockeries of so-called scholasticism of the modern world that has already de-socialized man from being 'men'. The plundered planet as ours is, awaits a revaluation of consciousness through fulness in education. Hence, social change, and social excellence. How can this social excellence be brought about ? Tagore has a unique socio-philosophical approach which he practically experimented in his own centre of social learning and institute of rural development at Sriniketan. As he elucidates :

We are born conscious of one truth, which is for us the background to our knowledge of all other truths. It is the truth about *myself*, and consists of an inner reality with certain outer manifestations. The manifestations can be proved and measured, but not the inner reality. or that deeper self, which gives to the outer manifestations their unity. There have been people to whom the diverse facts about the movements of my conscious or outer self are all this is real, but not the deeper truth within me, which is one. It requires no help from logic for me to realize the *Satyam*, the Truth, that One exists who not only comprehends all the facts of my life, but who transcends them.

—Rabindranath Tagore : "The Philosophical Approach to Sriniketan", incorporated in L.K. Elmhirst : *Rabindranath Tagore* : *Pioneer in Education,* Visva-Bharati 1961, pp. 85-86.

The belief in transcendance of individual excellence towards the welfare of every one in the society is what true education should ardently emphasize upon every action and every pattern of human behaviour. To expose 'the indwelling light of truth' of Oneness is the only way to realize the harmony of human consciousness :

By the indwelling light of this truth, I know that the world to which I belong, and which consists of an endless series of movements, has an inner truth of its own which is one, and which gives reality to the innumerable facts we know about the universe. We realize this inner truth, we experience *Ananda*, Joy, for through Joy we discover the eternal harmony of our own reality.

So often we ignore the real truth of a man and only deal with surface facts about him. The man who sells things to me is, for myself, a mere fact. The man whom I employ as my servant is a bundle of certain facts, all useful in the particular facts and circumstances of my life. Through such facts I find the satisfaction of many of my needs, but no joy. For joy comes only when we realize the harmony of the *Satyam*, or Truth, that is in us, with the *Satyam*, or Truth, that is in others, and, in this case, in my servant.

> But with regard to our loved ones, we are directly aware of the deeper truth which is constantly manifested through them in their outer life, because with them we more easily realize a mutual affinity. Their outer activity may hold no value for our own life's purposes, nay it may even be a hindrance. They have, however, an ultimate value for us in that they are, that they embody, an inner truth which is also within me.
>
> —*Ibid.*, p. 86.

Admittedly, the feeling for one and all—*Sarvanubhuti*—that education brings forth is the only way of social regeneration. That all wisdom is the sum total of experiences of world movements that form a vital part in one's being educated needs no explanation. To extend self-knowledge and to exert control over our self-seeking impulses would ultimately lead to desirable social development and social harmony. What we vainly boast of is the surface self that very often finds delight in pseudo-intellectual showmanship. As Oscar Wilde once described the social imbalances as outcomes of miseducation and belied intentions, we cannot but look askance at the modern aims and objectives of education that shakes hands with alienation, and of course, desolation.

While explaining the nature of modern civilization in relation to growing human apathy and ignorance, Tagore flashes out the true picture of the modern society of which we vainly boast :

> Civilisation today caters for a whole population of gluttons. An intemperance, which could safely have been tolerated in a few, has spread its contagion to the multitude. This universal greed, which now infects us all, is the cause of every kind of meanness, of cruelty and of lies in politics and commerce, and vitiates the whole human almosphere. A civilisation, which has attained such an unnatural appetite, must, for its continuing existence, depend upon numberless victims. These are being sought in those parts of the world where human flesh is cheap. In Asia and Africa a bartering goes on through which the future hope

and happiness of entire peoples is sold for the sake of providing some fastidious fashion with an endless supply of respectable rubbish.

The consequence of such a material and moral drain is made evident when one studies the condition manifested in the grossness of our cities and the physical and mental anaemia of the villages almost everywhere in the world. For cities inevitably have become important. The city represents energy and materials concentrated for the satisfaction of an exaggerated appetite, and this concentration is considered to be a symptom of civilisation. The devouring process of such an abnormality cannot be carried on unless certain parts of the social body conspire and organise to feed upon the whole. This is suicidal; but before a gradual degeneracy ends in death, the disproportionate enlargement of the particular portion looks formidably great. It conceals the starved paller of the entire body. The illusion of wealth becomes evident because certain portions grow large on their robbery of the whole.

—Rabindranath Tagore : Presidential Address under the auspices of the Visva-Bharati Sammilani at the Rammohan Library, Calcutta, July 28, 1922 published as "Introduction to 'The Robbery of the Soul' " in L.K. Elmhirst : *Poet And Ploughman*, Visva-Bharati, Calcutta, 1975, pp. 34-35.

Tagore did not overlook the vitiated atmosphere created by the so-called social prosperity through sham democracy where an individual's personality is altered through streamlined regimentation and mechanical role of sharing social responsibilities. Rather is he very much aware of that fulness of education for social change in which every individual in the society becomes conscious of eternal unity and truth. This will welcome a living relationship or a harmony of human consciousness. As he observes :

A living relationship in a physical, or in a social body, depends upon sympathetic collaboration and helpfulness between the various individual organs or members. When a perfect balance of intercharge begins to operate, a consciousness of unity develops that is no longer easy to obstruct. The resulting health or wealth are both secondary to this sense of unity which is the ultimate end and aim, and a creation in its own right. Whenever some sectarian ambition for power establishes a dominating position in life's republic, the sense of unity, which can only be generated and maintained by a perfect rhythm of reciprocity between the parts, is bound to be disturbed. In a society where the greed of an individual or of a group is allowed to grow uncontrolled, and is encouraged or even applauded by the populace, democracy, as it is termed in the West, cannot be truly realised. In such an atmosphere a constant struggle goes on among individuals to capture public organisations for the satisfaction of their own personal ambition. Thus democracy becomes like an elephant whose one purpose in life is to give joy rides to the clever and to the rich. The organs of information and expression, through which opinions are manufactured, and the machinery of administration, are openly or secretly manipulated by the prosperous few, by those who have been compared to the camel which can never pass through the needle's eye, that narrow gate that leads to the kingdom of ideals. Such a society necessarily becomes inhospitable, suspicious, and callous towards those who preach their faith in ideals, in spiritual freedom. In such a society people become intoxicated by the constant stimulation of what they are told is progress, like the man for whom wine has a greater attraction than food.

—*Ibid.*, p. 35.

To renew our vision of social change in a fresher gladness of awakening in course of education for fulness we have no way out but to be aware of the allowance of democracy in the joy ride for the clever and the rich and averting the strenuous path of unfolding the real joy and truth of humanity. The social complexities carefully camouflaged in awful affluence allow rich grounds for education to take the initiative in right earnest. Today's education must not fight shy of their crucial change. The colossal wastage of human energy in accelerating outer growth instead of the inner, in scientific and mechanical development instead of creative and critical consciousness for the welfare of the society, signifies the fact that whatever education contributes to the society is nothing else than making everyone consumer-oriented.

Admittedly, a consumer-oriented society simply consumes itself. True education is thus lost in the whirlpool of misunderstanding, affluence, greed and mutual hatred in the society, all ultimately leading to the doom of the creative mind. It is interesting to note in this connection how Tagore as a great foreseer of the erosion of human society made his invaluable note of warning against the peril of the human society exactly sixty-seven years ago :

> When the determination to augment private possession, and to enjoy exclusive advantage, runs ahead of the common good and of general happiness, the bond of harmony, which is the bond of creation, must give way and brothers must separate, nay, even become enemies.
>
> This passion of greed that rages in the heart of our present civilisation, like a volcanic flame of fire, is constantly struggling to erupt in individual bloatedness. Such eruptions must disturb man's creative mind. The flow of production which gushes from the cracks rent in society gives the impression of a hugely indefinite gain. We forget that the spirit of creation can only evolve out of our own inner abundance and so add to our true wealth. A sudden increase in the show of production of things tends to consume our resources and require us to build new storehouses. Our needs, therefore, which stimulate this increasing flow, must begin to observe the limitation of normal demands. If we go on stoking our demands into bigger and bigger flames the conflagration that results will no doubt, dazzle our sight, but its splendour will leave on the debit side only a black heap of charred remains. When our wants are moderate, the rations we each claim do not exhaust the common store of nature and the pace of their restoration

does not fall hopelessly behind that of our consumption. This moderation leaves us leisure to cultivate happiness, that happiness which is the artist's soul of the human world, and which can create beauty of form and rhythm of life. But man today forgets that the divinity within him is revealed by the halo of this happiness. The Germany of the period of Goethe was considered to be poverty stricken by the Germany of the period of Bismarck. Possibly the standard of civilisation, illuminated by the mind of Plato, or by the life of the Emperor Asoka, is underrated by the proud children of modern times who compare former days with the present age of progress, an age dominated by millionaires, diplomats and war lords. Many things that are of common use today were absolutely lacking in those days. But are the people that lived then to be pitied by the young of our day who enjoy so much more from the printing press but so much less from the mind ?

* * * * *

Man has been digging holes into the very foundations not only of his livelihood but of his life. He is now feeding upon his own body. The reckless waste of humanity which ambition produces is best seen in the villages where the light of life is gradually being dimmed, the joy of existence dulled, and the natural bonds of social communion are being shapped every day. It should be our mission to restore the full circulation of life's blood into these martyred limbs of society; to bring to the villages health and knowledge; a wealth of space in which to live, a wealth of time in which to work, to rest and enjoy mutual respect which will give them dignity; sympathy which will make them realize their kinship with the world of men, and not merely their position of subservience.

—*Ibid.*, pp. 36-39.

For a desirable and effective change of consciousness in the society, education must make room for an appropriate endeavour to negotiate the crisis of culture that has eaten up the vitalities of our society. We should be right now aware of the true objectives of culture that stand for the overall refinement of humanity. That true sociability is inseparably related to true culture can hardly be denied. The readiness of the mind and the sense organs of everyone in the society is the great outcome of true education that, again, represents true culture. As Tagore observes :

> Culture leads the mental attitudes of the whole man from deeper stratas towards success. By virtue of its influence man constantly attains all round success from the heart. By virtue of its influence, the devotion to achieve unobtrusive knowledge and the enthusiasm for performance of selfless activities turn out to be natural. True culture gives greater value to genuine courtesy than observing rituals mechanically. Its stricture is not the strategy of humility suitable for having the desirable end in dealing with mankind. A cultured man might inflict harm to himself but cannot make himself insignificant. He feels ashamed to thrust himself ahead by selfishly pushing all behind or preach himself with all showmanship. Whatever is mean or hypocritical pains him. As he has ardent relationship with whatever is best in art or literature or in the history of man he gets pleasure in honouring every type of proficiency. He can assess and forgive, he can see whatever is good even by surmounting the obstacles of clash of opinions. He feels himself deficient and weak in showing his entry towards others' success.
>
> —Rabindranath Tagore: "*Siksha O Sangskriti*" ("Education and Culture"), *Siksha*, Visva-Bharati, 1973, pp. 226-227.
>
> [Translated by me]

Of late, the crisis of culture has been deeply felt in the society where education enjoys fragmentation and allows disintegration in every affair of life. We are veering like the wings of a compass because our objectives are yet to be spelt out in terms of desirable synchronization between education and society or between culture and society in particular. From an even more comprehensive spectrum of education for social development in relation to exposure of global culture, Prof. Prem Kirpal's views are very suggestive and thought provoking :

The crisis of culture in the developing societies partakes of the larger crisis of our contemporary civilization. I believe that this crisis is composed of three main elements in the world situation today. In the first place, we are being overwhelmed, even being eliminated as persons, by a process of fragmentation, dominated by an obsession for analysis, mechanization and over-specialization. We see around us a continuing fragmentation of life, of man, and of knowledge, undermining the unity of living, the identity and integration of the individual, and the wholeness of truth, which is bigger than mere factual data and patches of knowlege. This process leads to uncertainty, confusion and loss of faith, and man becomes a helpless subject to his own computer. There is an urgent need for a fresh synthesis and a new vindication of the wholeness of man, of a more unified order in his inner and outer world, and of the basic and fundamental truths and values. We need a much greater and more conscious emphasis upon synthesis and convergence towards a new humanism.

The second element in the crisis of our times is that of a terrible unreality, a widening gulf between thought and action, which is even wider and more serious than the gap between material affluence and poverty. Splendid profession, majestic formulation and powerful manifestoes from the ruling establishments are daily manufactured and magnified by the manipulation of the media of communications. The abundance of thought is matched by a pathetic paucity of action; what is more dangerous is that it is accepted, even taken for granted, that what we profess will not be practised and what is promised is not intended to be fulfilled. In this state of unreality which verges on dishonesty, can we blame the youthful dissenters when they protest in anger and despair.

The insufficient stress on the moral and ethical element in promoting peace and development is the third feature of the deepening crisis. The pace of development has regressed sadly, the peace of the world remains apprently fragile and threatened, the violation of human rights is greater than their loud proclamation, and violence looms larger with the increase of self-centeredness, indifference and greed.

—Prem Kirpal, Culture and Development—The Incipient Crisis", *Cultures*, UNESCO, Vol. III, No. 4, 1976, pp. 83-84.

Nearly eighty years ago, exactly on August 19, 1912 Tagore, while in Glocestershire, wrote about the then prevailing conditions of the Indian society and her social imbalances due to aimlessness in education and pointed out specific avenues to avert this crisis of civilization :

> We have no clarity in our life. Nowhere in our country is there any specific indication of what we can be or how far we can aspire. The authority to desire makes the power of man forceful. In the caressing of Nature there cannot be any wastage of energy. For this, where there is no hope, force bids farewell from there. In science it is said that when sighted animals live for long in cages, they lose vision. As Nature cannot tolerate the inconsistency of power of vision in the absence of light so it is unbearable for her to have power *sans* hope. For this when there is no way out to flee away in the face of danger, the power to run away also becomes arrested.
>
> —Rabindranath Tagore : "*Lakshya O Siksha*" ("Aims and Education"), *Siksha*, Visva-Bharati, 1973, p. 130.
>
> [Translated by me]

That education is not playing its desirable role for social change has been forcefully hammered by Tagore from the above points of vicissitudes in our aims of education. What education should crave for is to allow every individual to be inquisitive and dynamic in his approach to the welfare of the society in which he lives. Rather than carelessly cultivating the energy of hopelessness and artificialities through sham education, let every individual utilize his inherent power of infinite potentialities to bring about necessary, rapid and worthwhile social change. Tagore makes a very excellent exposition in this regard from the standpoint of human power and aspiration :

> ...If the sphere of hope becomes great, the power of mankind also becomes great and thrives. The power then gets its power to visualize its avenues distinctly and forcefully steps on. Any society that can afford the greatest thing to mankind is the greatest hope. It is not that everyone in the society achieves complete success of that aspiration. But as there is always an inclination towards that hope directly or indirectly, everyone's power can proceed till its end. It is the most important thing for a nation. There is no value of population; but the power and resources whatsoever of most of the people of the society are being utilized and are not buried in the ground—that is prosperity. Where power is dynamic, goodness prevails there. Where wealth becomes living and are being utilized, therein lies grandeur.
>
> —*Ibid.*, pp. 130-131.
> [Translated by me]

In our education, the individual is crippled in course of studies that adorn, in the end, an individual with degrees, diplomas and certificates with practically meaningless abstractions. Society, in fact, gets no benefit at all. The seeds of alienation are nursled in dumb isolation. An individual neither remains an individual nor becomes social in such type of education as it does not allow him to play a significant role in the society to sacrifice himself for the greater cause of mankind. Tagore highlights this distorted aim of education very characteristically :

> Education is not something alienated from life. What we would be and what we would learn are closely interlinked.

* * * * *

We have nothing much to want. The society is not beckoning us towards greater activities, or greater sacrifices. It does not want from us any account except maintenance of rules and regulations related to day to day bare livelihood.

** ** ** **

As we fail to visualize life in broader perspectives, we naturally fail to recall our role to broaden or sacrifice our life. Whatever we think over that verges on bookish thought, whatever work we are to do becomes a mere imitation of others.

—*Ibid*., p. 131.
[Translated by me]

Freedom for fulness of education as Tagore emphasizes is both mandatory and purposful for social orientation. An individual becomes truly educated when he wholeheartedly involves himself towards greater cause of the society. It is high time for him to dispel all illusions related to social progress. Mere apeing of socio-cultural abnormalities writ large in the face of macabre modernity leads to moratorium in the name of education.

The freedom to be true to oneself in order to be true to the society in which one lives necessitates freedom in the process of education. Let there be an open avenue of excellence to be manifested in diverse activities of the society. Let education allow everyone in the society to be true to each other in all respects and in all directions of the society. The involvement of the individual to the society must come from within and not thrust from outside. Meanwhile, let education create an ardent atmosphere of mutual harmony and understanding between man and man in the society.

The role of mass education in the upbringing of the society is perhaps more than a misnomer since the primary distinction between man and man at least from the point of imbalance in status and standard of living more often than not remains ignored in the so-called crusade against social disparities. Our goal of education is not in tune with that of our society nor do we ever care for it in spite of the fact that liberation from social disparities cannot await mandates extrinsically. Involvement in social changes, be it through education or through any other discipline, must primarily be germinated in the granary of genuine love for society.

The misfortune that looms large in our fragmented and bewildered policies on education is one of compartmentalized policies encapsulated in freeze programmes. In mass education, for instance, so much of utilitarian principles and strategies are chalked out and implemented as to ignore the essential purpose of education to become oneself in the society. As a result, mass education turns into a mess of public money bungled away in buffooned bolsters. It is a rare case in education in the global society even now to see a community of persons involved in the same way of social devotion as ones blessed with normal upbringing in education. When education becomes a proxy for patchwork, society wails in silence.

Perhaps somewhere in the heartland of ours even now harbours the ship of recovery. We will have to launch our expedition for social change through fulness in education. But how ? Here's the answer from Tagore :

> In our country there are emotional outbursts to a great extent. We do not involve ourselves unintoxicatedly in the celebration of our functions. Accept the responsibilities of the country knowing everything like incompleteness, ignorance and nuisance of the country by means of dispelling the attachment to unrealities in the light of bright intelligence like men. Where, in reality, our fortune betrays and humiliates us everyday, the effort at making oneself unaware of self-composed pride is the poor indication of the feeble mind. Prior to beginning any real work, one should have to know and admit that our disaster deeply lies inherently in our society and manners, in our habits and abnormalities in intelligence.
>
> ** ** **
>
> Today our expedition is against our inherent self-enmities. We will have to wholeheartedly strike at the very

foundation of the fort of ignorance built in a period of many centuries.

** ** **

We can awake the best of others by awakening the best within ourselves.

—Rabindranath Tagore : "*Chhatrasambhasan*." ("Address to the Students"), *Siksha*, Visva-Bharati, 1973, p. 259.
[Translated by me.]

Are we prepared to awake ourselves through education for a greater and worthier social change ?

TAGORE'S CONCEPT OF MAN

Man today stands at the cross-roads of identity and extinction. The maladies of the modern man are legion. He suffers within himself and allows these sufferings to persist because he feels he has no alternative. Often these sufferings are fabricated for a camouflaged approach to intellectualism—a craze from which he cannot evade himself. Again, he makes allowance to sufferings to thrive because he has a false notion of erosion of consciousness and *Kenosis* or emptying the mind which is, in reality, a genuine outcome of endless devotion to know oneself from every avenue of erudition and experience.

A certain sense of ukase in self-negation and self-surrender be it through peculiar pursuits, has for man become not only a fashion but also a devotion and a norm. The ways are diverse and man's conquest of himself shakes hands with an excess of disappointment and disillusion.

Unlike other thinkers and humanists, Tagore looks at man both from within and from outside. The hollowness of man marooned in crisis of character and civilization did not avert his attention. What ails Tagore is the failure of man to feel the inner pulse of action, the great truth within. As a greater species of creation, he thinks that the great power within man ignites him to play his role for emancipation of himself through emancipation of the whole of mankind.

As for himself, Tagore shows the way in a very unassuming fashion. The way of freedom for man is, as he introspects, that of the feeling of the divine presence of God who makes him ever aware of his own pitfalls and disallows by himself any favour which might tarnish the greatness of man as man. The constraints are, therefore, welcome, since the identity of the unison between the Creator and man remains unhampered. Moreover, the debts incurred to the Lord are endless and unrepayable. As he muses on :

> Obstinate are the trammels, but my heart aches when I try to break them.
>
> Freedom is all I want, but to hope for it I feel ashamed. I am certain that priceless wealth is in thee, and that thou art my best friend, but I have not the heart to sweep away the tinsel that fills my room.
>
> The shroud that covers me is a shroud of dust and death; I hate it, yet hug it in love.
>
> My debts are large, my failures great, my shame secret and heavy; yet when I come to ask for my good, I quake in fear lest my prayer be granted.
>
> —Rabindranath Tagore : *Gitanjali*, Macmillan Pocket Tagore Edition, Macmillan & Co. Ltd., 1962, No.XX VIII, pp. 16-17.

The truth in man to grow instinctively in the face of all obstructions is what glorifies man as man. And so Tagore considers apology to be a defeat and awakening of consciousness in a renewed vision of advancement a great march of man. As a child of God, man cannot but be treated with respect. Dan Wilson highlights this Christian belief in the uniqueness of man for his incomparable intrinsic worth and remarks ;

> The universal is ever seeking its consummation in the unique and the desire we have to keep our uniqueness intact is really the desire of the universe acting in us.
>
> —Dan Wilson : *Promise of Deliverance*, Pendle Hill, Wallingford, U.S.A., 1951, p. 20.

Tagore deeply feels the inadequacies of this 'uniqueness' of man in our system of education that fails to bring about necessary changes to realize the immense potentialities of man as man. The real concept of man as he defines from the pedogogical point of view is also very poignant and pulsating.

As an ardent educationist, he feels that the very nature of man in his exceptional power of adjustability has yet been properly adhered to by a schizophrenic society :

> For various unavoidable reasons in the history of man wars sometimes take place, sometimes, again, peace prevails; the spate of wealth and affluence sometimes occur or at times its ebb tide flows. Sometimes man becomes frenzied in his own strength while at times he becomes overwhelmed with the sense of his own helplessness. Under such circumstances, when man is leaning towards one side, it is the true education for him to give a great pull from the other side. When the nature of man remains strong and lively, he selects the harmony of balance by means of an easy force that comes from within his own self. The man who has control over his own body, naturally adjusts himself, when he wants to negotiate a jolt from one end, by balancing on the other side. But an intoxicated person dwindles with a little jolt and remains so at that place. The strategies for educating the children in Europe are changing from within. The more their minds are becoming aware of diverse ideas and knowledge through association of experiences, the more are the rapid changes taking place in their avenues.
>
> —Rabindranath Tagore : "*Sikshavidhi*" ("Principles of Education"), *Siksha*, Visva-Bharati, 1973, pp. 124-125.
>
> [Translated by me]

That the course of education is to be directed in accordance with the diverse avenues of the mind so that the real 'man' in man comes out in all spontaneity and significantly plays its part in the history of human civilization, is an invaluable contribution to the concept of man. Tagore highlights this concept from his intense study of man as a socio-cultural being. The true concept of the nature of man, as he thinks, is in realization of steadfastness to truth and cultivation of courtesy, simplicity and other virtues that mirror the true culture of man as a social being. The dehumanization of man as seen in all ugliness in all affairs of life has pained Tagore. The real picture of the crisis of character that has been eating up the inner vitalities of man does not avert his foresight :

> We do not feel slightly ashamed to admit that it is enough to go on maintaining the external status alone. Even we do not hesitate to say that we can do whatever we would practically like to do but there is no harm if we do not admit it publicly. This type of practice in dishonesty is to be accepted by man under trying circumstances. This is because when your reverence has taken a different course, the people of the society do not feel ashamed by taking recourse to dishonest means in case the society stifles the conventions in the same place As there are very few heroic personalities amongst people this state of affairs goes on. Therefore, where the punishment for admitting truth in public is intolerably great, one cannot consider it to be a crime to take recourse to hypocrisy.
>
> —Rabindranath Tagore : "*Sikshavidhi*" ("Principles of Education"), *Siksha*, Visva-Bharati, 1973, pp. 126.
>
> [Translated by me]

Encaged in which-how position in the society, man today is lost within man. The best of man as Tagore rightly thinks suffers terribly because the best of his thoughts die unborn and unexpressed. This has been the regular and unavoidable scene in almost all the educational institutions and nearly everywhere in the society where hypocrisy is honoured and heroism of manliness of character is hackled and maimed. The growth of human personality is thus stunted right from the beginning of efflorescence of uniqueness. The concept of man as a unique living being cannot be allowed to be choaked in chaos, but the education of man allows chaos in character-development in our so-called educational institutions that hardly pay attention to exercise of individual uniqueness. For a man to be a 'man', his role of taking part in eternity by means of his uniqueness is infinite.

It is because things happen but once that the individual takes partakes in eternity. For the individual with his inextinguishable uniqueness is engraved in the heart of all and lies forever in the lap of the timeless as he who is committed thus and not otherwise. Uniqueness is the essential good of man that is given to him to unfold.

—Martin Buber : *The Legend of the Baal-Shem*, Translated by Maurice S. Friedman, Harper, New York, 1955, p. 41.

To unfold oneself in order to realize the 'man' in oneself is the only reason why Tagore thought of a school for exercise and emancipation of uniqueness. The bondage of uniqueness as he deeply felt while he was a school boy, is the bondage of humanity. The 'man' in a man suffers most when this bondage dominates over him. Tagore wants to give freedom to have a significant role in the concept of man. Looking back to his horrid boyhood days in schools, he analyses the role of freedom in being oneself, 'man' as a man should be :

Looking back upon those moments of my boyhood days, when my mind seemed to float poised upon a large feeling of the sky, of the light, and to mingle with the brown earth in its glistening glass, I cannot help believing that my Indian ancestry had left deep in my being the legacy of its philosophy : the philosophy which speaks of fulfilment through a harmony with all things. For good or for evil such a harmony has the effect of arousing a great desire in us to seek our freedom, not in the man-made world but in the depth of the universe, and makes us offer our reverence to the divinity inherent in fire, water and trees, in everything moving and growing. The founding of my school had its origin in the memory of that longing for freedom, the memory which seems to go back beyond the sky-line of my birth.

Freedom in the mere sense of independence has no content, and therefore no meaning. Perfect freedom lies in the perfect harmony of relationship which we realize in this world—not through our response to it in *knowing* but in *being*. Objects of knowledge maintain an infinite distance from us who are the knowers. For knowledge is not union.

> Therefore the farther world of freedom awaits us where we reach truth, not through feeling it by our senses, or knowing it by reason, but through the union of perfect sympathy.
>
> —Rabindranath Tagore : "A Poet's School" from *Rabindranath Tagore : Pioneer in Education* by L.K. Elmhirst, Visva-Bharati, 1961, pp. 51-52.

To attain harmony within oneself is to be a 'man' within and to be a 'man' within is to be christened with 'the harmony of relationship which we realize in this world' by means of our *being*. As the Buddha says,

> Be ye lamps unto yourselves,
> Be your own reliance.
> Hold to the truth within yourselves as to the only lamp.
>
> —Quoted by Victor Gollancz : *Man and God*, Houghton Mifflin & Co., Boston, U.S.A., 1951, p. 395.

Highlighting the importance of freedom for the desirable outcome of the 'man' in children, Tagore recalls his boyhood days when he was in utter banishment of the soul in him that barred all doors of emancipation of the inner spirit in him :

> For our perfection we have to be vitally savage and mentally civilized : we should have the gift to be natural with Nature and human with human society. The misery which I felt was due to the crowded solitude in which I dwelt in a city where man was everywhere, with never a gap for the immense non-human. My banished soul sitting in the civilized isolation of town-life cried within me for the enlargement of the horizon of its comprehension. I was like the tornaway line of a verse, always in a state of suspense, while other line, with which it rhymed and which could give it fulness, was smudged away, into some misty, undecipherable distance. The inexpensive power to be happy which, along with other children, I brought with me to this world, was being constantly worn away by friction

> with the brick-and-mortar arrangement of life, by mechanical habit and a code of customary respectability.
>
> —Rabindranath Tagore : "A Poet's School" from *Rabindranath Tagore : Pioneer in Education* by L.K. Elmhirst, Visva-Bharrti, 1961, pp. 52-53.

The sense of desolation from which Tagore suffered in his boyhood days, destroys the inner 'man' which is the real man. For fulness of being, man must make a continual rediscovery *to be* from what he *is*. This, indeed, is the goal of education, the goal of *being*. In the words of D.H. Lawrence,

> Every individual is to be helped, wisely, reverently, towards his own natural fulfilment......Every man shall be himself, shall have every opportunity to come to his own intrinsic fulness of being...The final aim is not to *know* but to *be*.
>
> —Quoted by G.H. Bantock : *Freedom and Authority in Education : A Criticism of Modern Cultural and Educational Assumptions*, Faber & Faber, London, 1953, p. 164.

In order to draw out the 'man' in children, the inherent uniqueness, Tagore also aims at *being* in the backdrop of knowledge and erudition. From this psychological point of view, his analysis of the nature of children provides ample proof of his crystallized concept of man :

> Children have their active subconscious mind which, like the tree, has the power to gather its food from the surrounding atmosphere. For them the atmosphere is more important than rules and methods, building appliances, class teachings and text books. The earth has her mass of substance in her land and water. But, if I may be allowed figurative language, she finds her inspiration of freedom, the stimulation of her life, from her atmosphere. It is, as it were, the envelopment of her perpetual education. It brings from her depth responses in colours, and perfume, music and movement, her incessant self-revelation, continual

wonders of the unexpected. In his society man has the diffuse atmosphere of culture always about himself. It has the effect of keeping his mind sensitive to his racial inheritance, to the current of influences that come from tradition; it makes it easy for him unconsciously to imbibe the concentrated wisdom of aged. But in our educational organizations we behave like miners, digging only for things substantial, through a laborious process of mechanical toil : and not like a tiller of the soil, whose work is in a perfect collaboration with Nature, in a passive relationship of sympathy with the atmosphere.

—Rabindranath Tagore : "A Poet's School", from *Rabindranath Tagore : Pioneer in Education* by L.K. Elmhirst, Visva-Bharati, 1961, pp. 63-64.

How to develop the yearning for knowing the inner 'man' to be inspired with the inherent uniqueness ? Tagore has a very positive answer. It is to create an atmosphere of understanding and appreciating the inner 'man' through cultivation of sensibilities inherent in everyone :

...I tried to create an atmosphere in my institution, giving it the principal place in our programme of teaching. For atmosphere there must be for developing the sensitiveness of soul, for affording mind its true freedom of sympathy. Apathy and ignorance are the worst forms of bondage for man; they are the invisible walls of confinement that we carry round us when we are in their grip. In educational organizations our reasoning faculties have to be nourished in order to allow our mind its freedom in the words of truth, our imagination for the world of human relationship. This last is even more important than learning the geography of foreign lands.

—*Ibid.*, p. 64.

The education for the sensitive 'man', the man who continually discovers himself from intrinsic as well as extrinsic points of view, is yet to begin anew in our educational institutions. The way to be nearer to one's 'man' in oneself is the way of transcendence—the way of the lost soul to be recovered. In the words of James Baldwin,

> The paradox of education is precisely this—that as one begins to become conscious one begins to examine the society in which he is being educated. The purpose of education, finally, is to create in a person the ability to look at the world for himself, to make his own decisions*** The obligation of anyone who thinks of himself as responsible is to examine society and try to change it—and to fight it—at no matter what risk. This is the only hope society has. This is the only way societies change.
>
> —James Baldwin, "A Talk to Teachers", *Saturday Review*, December 21, 1963, p. 42.

Unlike Baldwin, Tagore becomes more specific in his concept of man, to become oneself, in his pin-pointed, glaring, pregnant and vibrant approach to the development of inner sensibilities in children :

> **Let no such superstition be nurtured in the minds of children that learning is reading books. It is to be known at every step that the treasures of books are accumulated from the storehouse of Nature, and this should be, and we have also the authority to have it in the same way. As the disturbances of books are taking place to a great extent, I would like to assert it more emphatically.
>
> —Rabindranath Tagore : "*Avaran*", *Siksha*, Visva-Bharati, 1973, p. 75.
>
> [Translated by me]

The real 'man' lost in the melee of mechanization, automation and artificialities indicates a massacre of human sensibilities. The inner worth of man is duped in undesirable silence. The choaked voice of man lost in the whirlwind of debased humanity finds joy nowhere. Education—lifeless, dull, mechanical—awaits de-education to be dawned in a new perfume of promise. The ascent of man is in his excellence in evaluating himself. As Tagore muses with endless askesis of prayer,

Amar prane r majhe jeman Kare
Naache tomar pran
Amar preme temni tomar premer
Vahuk na tufaan
Raser varisane
Taare milaao savaar sane,
Anjali mor chhapiye diye
Hok se tomar daan
Amar hriday sada amar majhe
Vandi haye thaake.
Tomar aapan paashe niye tumi
Mukta karo taake
Jeman tomar taara
Tomar phoolti jeman dhaara,
Temni taare tomar karo
Jeman tomar gaan.

Just as in my heart of hearts
Your heart does dance
Let the tornado of your love blow in abundance
In my heart
With the shower of juice
Let it be in unison with all
Overflowing my offerings
Let it be your gift.
My heart remains imprisoned
Within me.
Take it beside you and deliver it.
Just as your stars
Your flowers as well
So let it be yours very own
As your song

—Rabindranath Tagore : *Geetimalya. Rabindra-Rachanavali*, Government of West Bengal, Calcutta, 1980, Vol. II, No. 110, p. 359.

[Translated by me]

The release of the obsessions within and unison with the infinite is what Tagore highlights as the essential concept of man. It is a submission of man to the altar of the Eternity, the Ever Present that makes man worthy of himself. This is, indeed, a marvellous experience tinged in myriad emotions and sensibilities of life. It knows no denial nor even any rejection in oneself because the Ever Present is always there to show His manifold manifestation. The 'man' in man cannot but salute this inherent change with the change of the Lord of the heart. The song echoes the very core of the 'man' in man born of contemplation synchronized with heavenly contentment :

Mor sandhyay tumi sundarveshe eshechho
Tomay kari go namaskar.
Mor andhakarer antare tumi heshechho
Tomay kari go namaskar.
Ei namra nirav soumya gabhir akashe
Tomay kari go namaskar
Ei Santa sudhir tandranivid vatase
Tomay kari go namaskar.
Ei Klanta dharar shyamalanchal aasane
Tomay kari go namaskar.
Ei Stavdha tarar mouna-mantra-bhasane
Tomay kari go namaskar.
Ei Karma-ante nibhrita panthasalate
Tomay kari go namaskar.
Ei Gandha-gahan sandhya-kusum-malate
Tomay kari go namaskar.

Thou hast come in lovely apparel in the evening,
I salute Thee.
Thou hast smiled in my heart of darkness,
I salute Thee
In this sky humble and silent beautiful and deep,
I salute Thee
In this air gentle and very calm and dense in drowsiness,
I salute Thee.
In this green seat of the tired earth,
I salute Thee.

In this silent chanting speech of the dumb stars,
 In salute Thee.
In this secluded inn at the end of work,
 I salute Thee.
In this garland of evening flowers with the feast of fragrance,
 I salute Thee.

—Rabindranath Tagore : *Geetimalya, Rabindra-Rachanavali*, Government of West Bengal, Calcutta, 1980, Vol. II, No. 112, p. 360.

[Translated by me]

To be one with the world with all its diversities is what Tagore defines as the ideal concept of man. Here the distinction between the self and the non-self or more specifically between the world and man merges in unison; otherwise, we would, as he confidently asserts, never reach truth from untruth. As he remarks, taking the above assertion as a hypothesis,

> ***there would have been absolute misery and unmitigated evil in this world. Then from untruth we never could meet truth, and from sin we never could hope to attain purity of heart; then all opposites would ever remain opposites, and we could never find a medium through which our differences could ever lend to meet.
>
> —Rabindranath Tagore : *Sadhana*, Visva-Bharati, p. 105.

While defining the endless power of the Eternal spirit that remains in unison with man, Tagore makes a revolutionary approach to the oneness of things that highlights the glory of man. In his characteristic exposition of this revolutionary fact, the concept of man takes an altogether new dimension :

> The text of our everyday meditation is the *Gayatri*, a verse which is considered to be the epitome of all the Vedas. By its help we try to realise the essential unity of the world with the conscious soul of man; we learn to perceive the unity held together by the one Eternal Spirit, whose power creates the earth, the sky, and the stars, and at the same time irradiates our mind with the light of a conscious-

ness that moves and exists in unbroken continuity with the outer world.

—*Ibid.*, p. 9.

Rising on the dawn of the brightness of brilliance, man, as Tagore thinks, leaves off all his vain aspirations and merges in the Eternal Spirit with all the totality. The march of man is always a sacrifice of the self to be in constant companionship of the ultimate Beneficiary. As the *Iśopanisad* says :

Vāyur anilam amrtam
athedaṁ bhasmāntaṁ śarīram
Om krato smara krtam smara
Krato smara kṛtaṁ smara.

Let this temporary body be burnt into ashes, and let the air of life be merged with the totality of air. Now, O my Lord, please remember all my sacrifices, and because you are the ultimate Beneficiary, please remember all that I have done for you.

Śrī Iśopanisad, 17.

[Translated by A.O. Bhaktivedanta Swami Prabhupada, *Śrī Iśopanisad*, Iskon Press, 38, North Beacon Street, Boston, Massachusetts, 1969, pp. 86-87.]

As every man's soul is of infinite value, Tagore believes that every man should be always better than what he is at present. The continual moulding of man in the form of shaping his acts through discipline of mind is the stepping stone of excellence or the assent of man. How can he best formulate himself ? As Tagore thinks, a man in the true sense of the term knows how to train his passions to be the servants of his will and how to endear truth at all costs, honour goodness in every affair of life and share sympathy with one and all. The poverty of mind is the greatest enemy of man and so whatever endeavour is directed towards elimination of poverty from the mind would ultimately end in effulgence of excellence. Such an excellence, as Tagore profoundly believes, upholds man as the true image of God :

> Man is the image of God. So, like God, man is also endowed with form and formlessness. Form is man's ego while formlessness is his soul. The soul and the ego are as much beyond together and indispensable, to each other as the Infinite is related to the finite. Like God, man is also endowed with three natural powers—willing, knowing and feeling. Just as forms of the world are marching to the formless, so the ego of man is meant for the fulfilment of the spirit. This means that man should develop his willing, his knowing and his feeling in such a way that they can assert the glory of man's spirit. The criterion of the success of the inherent powers of man is : whether man's willing, feeling and knowing conform to those of God. When man merges his individual will into the will of God, his knowledge into the knowledge of God and his love into God's love, he is thereby said to have asserted the rights of the spirit in him. At this stage, man feels that what he does is really the fulfilment of God's will through him; he knows then that, like his own self, all selves are related to God. The discovery of integral relationship between God and all selves, introduces him to his natural relationship with all selves. So love of God on his part develops into love for all selves. For Tagore, God is man's God and the world of God is man's world. So love for humanity is the indispensable destiny of man, because love for humanity is nothing but love for God.
>
> —Siddheswar Bhattacharya : "Religion of a Poet," *The Calcutta Municipal Gazette*, Tagore Birth Centenary Volume, Supplement Issue, Vol. LXXV, No. 21, p. 114.

The concept of man so related to God brings forth another Tagorean dimension of the uniqueness of man. The endless endeavour of man to be in unison with God points towards another truth. It is oneness of man and God. As Radhakrishnan explains,

> With the annihilation of the ego comes the fulfilment of love. The self-centered life becomes God-centered. Man shall not see God and live, goes the saying. Certainly not.

So long as he is man he cannot see Him. When he sees Him he ceases to be man. Before that vastness and splendour man's individuality shrinks and crumbles into dust. The all-dwelling love invades, submerges, and overwhelms the individual consciousness. The whole individual—body, mind, and soul—is given up to God.

—S. Radhakrishnan : *The Philosophy of Rabindranath Tagore*, Good Companions Publishers, Baroda, 1961, p. 38.

Is man, then, lost in unison ? Does he really lose his identity ? Tagore has a very emphatic 'no' in response to this. For he believes that man is never a rival to God nor is he alienated from God. So he maintains and nursles his freedom of will in the comradeship with God :

God reigns in man and His grace radiates upon him to make of him what he should be. He kindles man's will with His will, his knowledge with His knowledge and his love with His love. Yet, man is not a helpless medium to be done upon by God. Man has free will. It is his free gift from God. So it is man's free choice to unfold himself before the powers of God. Man is not slave to God. They are two free beings that unite in the partnership of equality. God is related to man as father is to the son.

So, out of free choice, man seeks the help of God to develop himself. He gives expression to his will, with divine help, through incessant activity. His growing knowledge reveals that he is grounded in God. His growing feeling intensifies itself into love for God and therefore love of all men. The simultaneous operation of three powers in man renders him into a pilgrim. He is perpetually given to activity even after his physical death; he feels at every step that he is united with God; he finds his activity and knowledge prized by the realization of love for all.

—Siddheswar Bhattacharya : "Religion of a Poet," *The Calcutta Municipal Gazette*, Tagore Birth Centenary Volume, Supplement Issue, Vol. LXXV, No. 21, p. 114.

It would not be inappropriate to refer to Tagore's aims and objectives of his own Visva-Bharati, 'where', as he spells out the motto, 'the world makes its home in a single nest' : *Yatra Visvam bhavatyekanidam* :

To STUDY THE MIND OF MAN in its realization of different aspects of truth from diverse points of view.

To bring into more intimate relation with one another through patient study and research, the different cultures of the East on the basis of their underlying unity.

To approach the West from the standpoint of such a unity of the life and thought of Asia.

To seek to realize in a common fellowship of study the meeting of the East and the West, and thus ultimately to strengthen the fundamental condition of world peace through the establishment of free communication of ideas between the two hemispheres.

And with such ideals in view to provide at Santiniketan a Centre of Culture where research into and study of the religion, literature, history, science and art of Hindu, Buddhist, Jain, Islamic, Sikh, Christian, and other civilizations may be pursued along with the culture of the West, with that simplicity in externals which is necessary for true spiritual realization, in amity, good fellowship and co-operation between the thinkers and scholars of both Eastern and Western countries, free from all antagonisms of race, nationality, creed or caste and in the name of the One Supreme Being who is *Santam Sivam Advaitam*.

—Rabindranath Tagore : "Aims and Objects", Santiniketan Vidyalaya (1901-1961), Visva-Bharati, 1961, p. 3.

What a piece of man in the Tagorean concept of man !

RABINDRANATH TAGORE AND SRI AUROBINDO : A QUEST FOR MYSTIC IDENTITIES

The way of beyonding of consciousness is the way of return to the roots. Mysticism, the only way of beyonding of consciousness, is the serene grace of the All Beautiful. To be an eternal partner to the play of the All Beautiful making myriad manifestations in man in his innermost consciousness is to harmonize the inner visions by means of perfume of promise and perfection. What are the promises of man to be kept with ardent devotion ? What are the items of consciousness within to be well nourished for perfection ? How to evolve and how to transcend from the present state of *being* to the future promise of *becoming* ? Mysticism has a definite say.

From truth to love and from love to light, mysticism has a grand journey. Both Rabindranath Tagore and Sri Aurobindo make adventures of their own towards beyonding of consciousness. Both have almost identical patterns of mystic imageries seeking the All Beautiful with every turn of inwardness of vision. In this serene involvement of the celebration of inner consciousness where man-God-man axis is in unison with the beauty of silence and purity of truth, while Tagore makes emotion crystallized in consciousness, Sri Aurobindo gives devotion the dimension of excellence in inwardness.

To carry the secret order of man's cosmic intentions is the source point of mysticism. Tagore goes in to the heartland of consciousness in delight and love tinged with the fabric of nature and comes out in poignance and mystic grandeur, meeting the Light of his life. The aroma of this meeting is attuned in *ektara*, the muse being an eternal source of mystic enjoyment. Sri Aurobindo beholds with his mind from its 'veiled sub-conscious state' the sombre state of a *sthita-prajna* to be in close comradeship with the Dervesh in his soul as a mystic *par excellence.*

To accept the All Beautiful as the 'truth' of life—the truth that enkindles the light of the mind is the mystic vision with which Tagore looks within and prepares for a beyonding of consciousness. The humble submission that the Poet makes to the 'Life of his life' is resonant with the perfume of future promise :

> Life of my life, I shall ever try to keep my body pure, knowing that thy living touch is upon my all limbs.
>
> I shall ever try to keep all untruths but from my thoughts, knowing that thou art that truth which has kindled the light of reason in my mind.
>
> I shall ever try to drive all evils away from my heart and keep my love in flower, knowing that thou hast thy seat in the inmost shrine of my heart.
>
> And it shall be my endeavour to reveal thee in my actions; knowing it is thy power that gives me strength to act.
>
> —*Geetanjali*, 4

For the ascent of consciousness, Sri Aurobindo has the vision of a 'bright archangel' that glooms over 'world-bare summits of being'. He has the same preparation for the Light of life like Tagore with an added poignance of experience in mystic sensibilities :

> As some bright archangel in vision flies
> Plunged in dream-caught spirit immensities,
> Past the long green crests of the seats of life,
> Past the orange skies of the mystic mind
> Flew my thought-self lost in the vasts of God
> Sleepless wide great glimmering wings of wind
> Bore the gold-red seeking of feet that trod
> Space and Time's mute vanishing ends. The face
> Lustred, pale-blue-lined of the hippogriff

Eremite, sole, daring the bourneless ways,
Over world-bare summits of being
Gleamed, the deep twilights of the world-abyss
Failed below Sun-realms of supernal seeing,
Crimson-white mooned oceans of pauseless bliss
Drew its vague heart-yearning with voice sweet.
Hungering, large-souled to surprise the unconned
Secrets white-fire-veiled to the lost Beyond,
Crossing power-swept silences rapture-stunned,
Climbing high far ethers eternal-sunned
Thought the great-winged wanderer paraclete
Disappeared slow-singing a flame-word rune.
Self was left, lone, limitless, nude, immune.

—"Thought the Paraclete".

With the blessings of the mystic vision as Sri Aurobindo exposes above, the voice of the 'living liberated person' echoes with the mystic promise : 'He acts and lives'. The enjoyment of infinity by the soul in the light of life makes everything secondary, for the mystic joy of the liberated soul of consciousness, as Sri Aurobindo believes, knows no end in the invigorating beauty of Nature :

Only to help God's forces to waiting Nature,
To help with wide-winged Peace her tormented labour
　And heal with joy her ancient sorrow,
　Casting down light on the inconscient darkness
He acts and lives, Vain things are mind's smaller motives
To one whose soul enjoys for its high possession
　Infinity and the sempiternal
　All his guide and beloved and refuge.

—"Jivanmukta".

For Tagore, the same mystic vision for the liberated soul as that of Sri Aurobindo takes an emotional aura of sensibilities to look at the desire of the heart, the beckoning of misery with the enkindling of 'the lamp of love' with the love of the All Beautiful. The Poet waits for 'a moment's flash of lightning, within himself as he is prepared to sing the mystic muse :

> Light, oh where is the light ? Kindle it with the burning fire of desire !
>
> There is the lamp but never a flicker
> Of a flame—is such thy fate, my heart ?
> Ah, death were better by far for thee !
>
> Misery knocks at thy door, and her message is that thy lord is wakeful, and he calls thee to the love-tryst through the darkness of night.
>
> The sky is overcast with clouds and the rain is ceaseless. I know not what this is that stirs in me—I know not its meaning.
>
> A moment's flash of lightning drags down a deeper gloom on my sight, and my heart gropes for the path to where the music of the night calls me.
>
> Light, oh where is the light ! Kindle it with the burning fire of desire ! It thunders and the wind rushes screaming through the void. The night is black as a black stone. Let not the hours pass by in the dark. Kindle the lamp of love with thy life.
>
> —*Geetanjali*, 27

The web of mystic enchantment with which Tagore endears himself also prepares him to welcome 'the innermost one'. The myriad changes that take place in his inner being is nothing but a prized transcendence,—a point of inner consciousness when there is self-oblivion in simplicity and beauty of the Eternal within him. The Poet so poignant in mystic experiences sings the welcome song with a profound sense of self-confidence :

> He it is, the innermost one, who awakens
> My being with his deep hidden touches.
> He it is who puts his enchantment
> Upon these eyes and joyfully plays on the chords of my heart in varied cadence of pleasure and pain.

He it is who weaves the web of this *maya* in evanescent hues of gold and silver, blue and green, and lets peep out through the folds his feet, at whose touch I forget myself.

Days come and ages pass, and it is ever he who moves my heart in many a name, in many a guise, in many a rapture of joy and of sorrow.

—*Geetanjali*, 72

Like Tagore, Sri Aurobindo also mystically muses on the 'ocean self enraptured and alone' :

My mind is awake in stirless trance,
  Hushed my heart, a burden of delight,
Dispelled is the senses' flicker-dance,
  Mute the body aureate with light.
O star of creation pure and free,
  Halo-moon of ecstasy unknown,
Storm-breath of the soul-change yet to be,
  Ocean self enraptured and alone.

—"Trance", *Collected Poems any Plays*, Vol. II, p. 280

What Sri Aurobindo says about the concepts of mystic and spiritual poetry may be recalled in connection with the above delightful experience of mystic vision :

I used the word mystic in the sense of a certain kind of inner seeing and feeling of things, a way which to the intellect would seem occult and visionary—for this is something different from imagination and its work with which the intellect is familiar. It was in this sense that I said I had not the mystic mind and vision. One can go far in the spiritual way, have plenty of spiritual experiences, spiritual knowledge, spiritual feelings, significant visions and dreams even without having this mystic mind and way of seeing things. So too one may write poetry from different planes or sources of inspiration and expressing spiritual feelings, knowledge, experiences and yet use the poetic intelligence as the thought medium which gives them shape in speech; such poems are not of the mystic type. One may be mystic in this sense without being spiritual—one may also be spiritual without being mystic; or one may be both spiritual and mystic in one.

—Sri Aurobindo : 'Mystic and Spiritual Poetry', *Letters of Sri Aurobindo* (Third Series), Sri Aurobindo Circle, Bombay 1949, p. 73.

The fusion of mystical and spiritually intense experiences as revealed in Sri Aurobindo's poetry of vision like "The Bird of Fire" marks a significant point of departure in mystico-spiritual sensibilities. For the sense of beauty that the poem creates along with its unparalleled imageries becomes lively in music, too. Here is the grand beginning :

Gold-white wings a-throb in the vastness, the bird of flame
Went glimmering over a sunfire curve to the haze of the west,
Skimming, a messenger-sail, the sapphire-summer waste of a soundless wayless burning sea.
Now in the eve of the waning world the colour and the splendour returning drifting through a blue-flicker air back to my breast.
Flame and shimmer staining the rapture-white form-vest of the waters of Eternity......

—"The Bird of Fire"

The voyage of 'the messenger-sail' on 'a wayless burning sea' as Sri Aurobindo muses on finds its partner in Tagore's 'last song' (obviously, never the last) in joy setting death and life—'the twin brothers'—in a dancing mood and making a dialogue with 'the open red lotus of pain'. Herein also the riot of imageries sweeps over the mind in the grand fashion-parade of beauty :

Let all the strains of joy mingle in my last song—the joy that makes the earth flow over in the riotous excess of the grass, the joy that sets the twin brothers, life and death, dancing over the wide world, the joy that sweeps in with the tempest shaking and waking all life with laughter, the joy that sits still with its tears on the open red lotus of pain, and the joy that throws everything it has upon the dust, and knows not a word.

—*Geetanjali*, 58

The grand ovation to light that Tagore gives in mystic vein along with the sky, the wind, the butterflies, the lilies and the jasmines brings forth a mystic contemplation in raptures of infinite mirth.

Light, my light, the world-filling light, the eye-kissing light, heart-sweetening light !

Ah, the light dances, my darling, at the centre of my life; the light strikes, my darling, the chords of my love; the sky opens, the wind runs wild, laughter passes over the earth.

The butterflies spread their sails on the sea of light. Lilies and jasmines surge up on the crest of the waves of light.

The light is shattered into gold on every cloud, my darling, and it scatters gems in profusion.

Mirth spreads from leaf to leaf, my darling, and gladness without measure. The heaven's river has drowned its banks and the flood of joy is abroad.

—*Geetanjali*, 57

The same sense of mystic vision is encountered in Sri Aurobindo who adorns imageries with the symbols of intense assertion of mysteries in the last stanza of "The Bird of Fire" :

Rich and red is thy breast, O bird, like the blood of a soul
climbing the hard crag-teeth world, wounded and nude,
A ruby of flame-petalled love in the silver-gold altar-vase
moon-edged night and rising day.
O Flame who art Time's last boon of the Sacrifice, offer-
ing flower held by the finite's gods to the Infinite.
O marvel-bird with the burning wings of light and the
unbarred lids that look beyond all space

One strange leap of thy mystic stress breaking
of the barriers
Mind and life, arrives at its luminous term thy flight,
Invading the secret clasp of the silence and crimson Fire
thou frontest eyes in a timeless Face.

—"The Bird of Fire"

The beauty of form and symbolic imagery that we encounter in legion in the mystic poem of both Tagore and Sri Aurobindo makes a new appeal to the consciousness of beyonding. Here is the picture of a mystic man 'a bright Persona of eternity' as Sri Aurobindo serenely states :

However long the night's hour, I will not dream
That the small ego and the person's mask
Are all that God reveals in our life-scheme,
The last result of Nature's cosmic task.
A greater presence in her bosom works :
Long it prepares its far epiphany;
Even in the stone and the beast the godhead lurks
A bright Persona of eternity,
It will burst out from the limit traced by Mind
And make a witness of the prescient heart;
It shall reveal even in the inert blind
Nature, long veiled in each inconscient part,
Fulfilling the occult magnificent plan,
The worldwide and immortal spirit in man.

—"The Hidden Plan"

The very earth—the Lotus Land of Purity—heralds the 'immortal spirit in man'. The world becomes a grand hinterland of man's fulfilment, never to be abandoned but always to be oriented in terms of cosmic enjoyment of the Eternal Now. It is the state of *nijantargatah* or endearing I to we and *vice versa* to have the mystic feeling and vision of William Blake

To see a world in a grain of sand
And Heaven in a wild flower,

Hold infinity in the palm of your hand
And Eternity in an hour.

To be an integral partner of the Eternal Now, Tagore makes an appeal to the Beautiful to accept him in eternal unison. As he muses on,

Ei labhinu sanga tava sundara he sundara.
Punya halo anga mama, dhanya halo antara
Aloke more chaksu duti mugdha haye uthlo phuti,
Hridgagane pavana halo sourabhete manthara sundara he sundara
Ei tomari parasaraage chitta halo ranjita,
Ei tomari milanasudha railo praane sanchita.
Tomar majhe emni kare navin kari lao je more
Ei janame ghatale more janma-jantantara sundara he sundara.

Thus have I received thy comradeship, Beautiful,
O Beautiful,
Virbuous became my limbs and blessed my heart
In light my two eyes did bloom in enchantment
The wind turned slow in the sky of my heart,
Beautiful. O Beautiful,
With this touch of thine my mind became colourful
With this drink of thy union did I treasure in my heart
Take me thus anew amidst thee
Thou didst make a life beyond life in me,
Beautiful, O Beautiful!

—Rabindranath Tagore : *Songs*, *Rabindra-Rachanavali*, Government of West Bengal, Calcutta, Vol. IV, No. 913, p. 378.

[Translated by me]

The same mystic note of unison with the All Beautiful is revealed in Sri Aurobindo's "Cosmic Consciousness" :

I have learned a close identity with all
Yet am by nothing bound that I become.
All sounds, all voices have become thy voice,
A secret harmony steals through the blind heart.

—"Cosmic Consciousness"

The mystic march of the individual, as Sri Aurobindo elucidates goes on eternally for the light 'that never was on sea or land' :

> The divine soul reproduces itself in similar liberated souls as the animal reproduces itself in similar bodies. Therefore whenever a single soul is liberated, there is a tendency to an extension and even to an outburst of the same divine self-consciousness in other individual souls of our terrestrial humanity and—who knows—perhaps even beyond the terrestrial consciousness. When shall we fix the limit of that extension ? Is it altogether a legend which says of the Buddha that as he stood on the threshold of Nirvana of the Non-Being, his soul turned back and took the vow never to make the irrevocable crossing so long as there was a single being upon earth undelivered from the knot of suffering, from the bondage of the ego ?
>
> —Sri Aurobindo : *The Life Divine*, Sri Aurobindo Ashram, Pondicherry, p. 40.

The preparation of the self to hear the mystic footsteps of the All Beautiful, as Tagore introspects, has the same promise in poignance of the deliverance from 'the bondage of the ego' in the pattern of the Buddha as Sri Aurobindo believes. Thus, the waiting for the 'golden touch' of the feet of the All Beautiful is the waiting of the Being to be a Non-Being in Light Eternal :

> Have you not heard his silent steps ? He comes, comes, ever comes.
>
> Every moment and every age, everyday and every night he comes, comes, ever comes.
>
> Many a song have I sung in many a mood of mind, but all their notes have always proclaimed, 'He comes, comes, ever comes,
>
> In the fragrant days of sunny April through the deep forest path, he comes, comes, ever comes
>
> In the rainy gloom of July nights on the thundering chariot of clouds he comes, comes, ever comes.

> In sorrow after sorrow it is his steps that press upon my heart, and it is the golden touch of his feet that makes my joy to shine.
>
> —*Geetanjali* 45

The pang of separation or the sorrow arising out of it brings forth for the Poet the mystic harmony of Infinity. A new arena of the vastness of emotions stands at the cathedral of sombreness in 'calmness of mind all passions spent' in the most Samsonian denouement :

> It is the pang of separation that spreads throughout the world and gives birth to shapes innumerable in the infinite sky.
>
> It is this sorrow of separation that gazes in silence all night from star to star and becomes lyric among rustling leaves in rainy darkness of July.
>
> It is this everspreading pain that deepens into loves and desires, into sufferings and joys in human homes; and this it is that ever melts and flows in songs through my poet's heart.
>
> —*Geetanjali*, 84

The symbols of emotions 'in the vividness of reality' of the mind, as Sri Aurobindo explains, find a poised mystic atmosphere in the above. What is considered to be the core of mystic vision of every mystic poem by him finds appropriate revelation in Tagore's mystic muse :

> Symbols may be of various kinds; there are those that are concealing images capable of intellectual interpretation but still different from either symbols or allegorical figures—and there are those that have a more definite intimate life of their own and are not conceptual so much as occultly vital in their significance; there are still others that need a psychic or spiritual or at least an inner and intuitive sight to identify oneself fully with their meaning. In a poem which uses conceptual symbols the mind is more active and the reader wants to know what it means to the mind; but as minds differ, the poet may attach one meaning to it and

the reader may find another, if the image used is at all an enigmatic one, not mentally clear and precise. In the more deeply symbolist—still more in the mystic—poem the mind is submerged in the vividness of the reality and any mental explanation falls far short of what is felt and lived in the inner vital or psychic response.* * * Mystic poetry can strike still deeper—it can stir the inmost and subtlest recesses of the life-soul and the secret inner mind at the same time; it can even, if it is of the right kind, go beyond these also to the pure inmost psychic.

—Sri Aurobindo : "Symbolic and Mystic Poetry", *Letters of Sri Aurobindo* (Third Series), Sri Aurobindo Circle, Bombay, 1949, pp. 77-79.

Bearing in mind the above concept of mystic poetry, let us have pure perception in the 'pure inmost psychic' :

Sometimes when our sight is turned within,
Earth's ignorant veil is lifted from our eyes;
There is a short miraculous escape.
This narrow fringe of clamped experience
We have behind meted out to us as life,
Our little walks, our insufficient reach
Our souls can visit in great lonely hours
Still regions of imperishable Light,
All-seeing eagle-peaks of power
And moon-flame oceans of swift and fathomless Bliss
And calm immensities of spirit Space.
In the unfolding process of the Self
Sometimes the inexpressible Mystery
Elects a human vessel of descent.

An exciting journey to 'the imperishable Light' within as Tagore makes heightens poetry to that magnificent grace by which the poet appears before us as 'a human vessel of descent :

Vajilo kahar veena madhur sware
Amar nibhrita nava jeevan-pare
Prabhatkamalsama phootilo hridaya mama
Kaar duti nirupam charan-tare

Jege othe sav sobha sav madhuri
Palake palake hiya pulake puri
Kotha hate samiran aane nava jagaran,
Paraner aavaran mochan kare
Laage vooke sukhe dukhe kata je vyetha
Kemane vujhaye kava na jaani katha.
Amar vaasana aazi tribhuvane uthe vaaji
Kaanpe nadi vanaraaji vedanabhare.

Whose *veena* played on in sonorous tunes
In my life new and serene
Like the morning lotus did my heart bloom
For the two decent feet I know not.
All grace makes up, all sweetness,
At every twinkling of eyes is the heart filled in joy
The gentle breeze brings forth new awakening
By dispelling the veil of the heart, I know not.
What a pain aches in the breast in happiness and sorrow
My words do fail to spell out.
My aspirations today ring in the world
In pangs of pain the river and the woods tremble.

—Rabindranath Tagore : *Songs, Rabindra-Rachanavali* Government of West Bengal, Calcutta, 1980, Vol. IV, No. 381, p. 188.

[Translated by me]

The poet has also an alternate suggestion to benignly voice forth in mystic muse :

Amare karo tomar veena, laho go laho tule
Uthive vaaji tantriraji mohan angule.
Komal tava kamalkare parash karo paran-pare
Uthive hiya gunjaria tava sravanmule
Kakhano sukhe kukhano dukhe kandive chahi tomar mukhe,
Charane padi rave nirave rahive jave bhule.
Keho na jane kee nava taane uthive geet sunya-paane,
Anander vaarata jaave ananter kule.

Make me thy *veena*, hold me, O hold me up.
The strings would tune on in lovely fingers.

With thy hands tender like the lotus, touch my heart
My heart would murmur in muse in thy ears
Sometimes in happiness, in sorrow sometimes would cry looking at thee
Silently would it lie at the feet in forgetfulness
None knows in what tuning anew would the muse march towards the vacant
The message of joy would move towards the shore of the endless.

—Rabindranarh Tagore : *Songs*, *Rabindra-Rachanavali*, Government of West Bengal, Calcutta, 1980, Vol. IV, No. 385, p. 189.

[Translated by me]

Perhaps Tagore and Aurobindo the two mystic bards of poignance believe in the truth of the Upanisadic dictum :

Yas tu sarvani bhūtāni
ātmani evānupaśyati
Sarva-bhūtesu cātmānaṁ
tato na vijugupsate.

—*Śrī Iśopaniṣad*, 6

A person who sees everything in relation to the Supreme Lord, and sees all entities as His part and parcel, and who sees the Supreme Lord within everything, never hates anything, nor any being.

[Translated by A.C. Bhaktivedanta Swami Prabhupada : *Śrī Iśopaniṣad*, ISKCON PRESS, Boston, Massachusetts, 1969, p. 33.

The absence of the Supreme Lord from the mystic bard makes an eternal surprise and a series of askance. The missing moments are agonies of immaturities. A matured mystic like Tagore cannot but muse in agonised sensibilities :

He came and sat by my side but I woke not.
What a cursed sleep it was, O miserable me !

He came when the night was still; he had his harp in his hands, and my dreams became resonant with its melodies.

Alas, why are my nights all thus lost ?
Ah, why do I ever miss his sight whose breath touches my sleep ?

—*Geetanjali*, 26

Simultaneously, let us hear the orphic voice of Sri Aurobindo :

Rose of God, vermilion stain on the sapphiers of heaven,
Rose of Bliss, fire-sweet, seven-tinged with the ecstasies seven !
Leap up in our heart of homeland, O miracle, O flame,
Passion-flower of the Nameless, but of the mystical Name.
Rose of God, great wisdom-bloom on the summits of being.
Rose of Light, immaculate core of the ultimate seeing !
Live in the mind of our earthhood, O golden Mystery, flower,
Sun of the head of the Timeless, guest of the marvellous Hour.

Rose of God, demask forces of Infinity, red icon of might,
Rose of Power, with thy diamond halo piercing the night !
Ablaze in the will of the mortal, design the wonder of the plan,
Image of Immortality, outbreak of the Godhead in man.
Rose of God, smitten purple with the incarnate divine Desire,
Rose of Life small, crowded with petals, colours' lyre !
Transform the body of the mortal like a sweet and magical rhyme;
Bridge our earthhood and heavenhood, make deathless the children of Time.
Rose of God, like a blush of rapture on Eternity's face,
Rose of Love, ruby depth of all being, fire-passion of Grace !

Arise from the heart of yearning that sobs in Nature's abyss,
Make earth the home of the wonderful and life Beatitude's kiss.

—Sri Aurobindo : "Rose of God", *Transformation and other Poems*, Sri Aurobindo Ashram, Pondicherry.

What a grand mystic ascent of Man !